270.8

The Evangelical Challenge

The Evangelical Challenge

By

MORRIS A. INCH

THE WESTMINSTER PRESS
Philadelphia

Scripture quotations are from the New American Standard Bible, © The Lockman Foundation 1960, 1962,
1963, 1968, 1971, 1972, 1973, 1975, and are used by
permission.

BOOK DESIGN BY DOROTHY ALDEN SMITH

First edition

Published by The Westminster Press®
Philadelphia, Pennsylvania

PRINTED IN THE UNITED STATES OF AMERICA

9 8 7 6 5 4 3 2 1

Library of Congress Cataloging in Publication Data
    Inch, Morris A   1925–
      The evangelical challenge.

      Bibliography: p.
      Includes index.
      1. Evangelicalism. I. Title.
    BR1640.I48   270.8'2   77–12310
    ISBN 0–664–24177–8

Contents

(Continued)

Part III   THE EVANGELICAL CONSCIENCE

Preface

There is likely no more significant religious development in our day than the massive resurgence of the evangelical faith. Yet its faddishness may obscure the facts concerning the movement.

I attempt to set forth the evangelical parameters in the discussion that follows. I begin with a brief historical survey and continue with the evangelical appeal to Christian orthodoxy, strategy, implementation, self-perception, and conscience. Some topics embrace more than one chapter, and each chapter concludes with a reader's summary of the critical points covered in the chapter.

Some readers will come as committed evangelicals, others with an affinity that had eluded them, still others with little favorable disposition. All, I hope, will benefit from a better appreciation of the evangelical perspective.

As for myself, I have mixed feelings about writing such a book. I freely admit to being an evangelical, but that fact seems inconsequential to confessing that I am a Christian. I suspect that this ambivalence generally characterizes evangelicals who only wish to accent their Christian faith by an appeal to evangelical convictions.

I acknowledge my evangelical mentors by way of dedicating the present volume. They are many and to mention a few by name would be to slight others. Regardless of whether they may have lacked in any particular, they have exhibited a personal commitment to Christ, a strong conviction as to their belief, and an appealing piety. As concerns the manuscript, I express my appreciation to Bonnie Ward for her editorial assistance and to Marian Filkin for her help in preparing the text.

M.A.I.

1

Evangelical Terrain

Is the evangelical movement just another fad? Washington news analyst Gary Willis labeled it today's "hot religious" development in a *Chicago Sun-Times* bicentennial article. He continued: "Serious people should be wary of religious fads, of yesterday's death of God and today's election of God. But the forces are there to be charted like moving hurricanes. Today's forecast is a spirit wind at high velocity."

Donald Bloesch also gets an evangelical hurricane reading: "The signs are unmistakable that evangelicalism today is experiencing a definite upturn."[1] Conferences, conservative church growth, publications, educational enterprise, renewal cells within old-line denominations, and the emergence of new evangelical groups point to a renewal of startling proportions.

This evangelical progress must seem puzzling to those accustomed to thinking of evangelicalism in terms of the sawdust trail—a chapter from America's past, the Methodist circuit rider, the Baptist revival—rather than a movement at the cutting edge of religious life today.

It is high time that we examine the genius of the evangelical cause. We should come to grips with the perspective on life held by evangelicals, their view on priorities, and the resources they sense to be at their

9

disposal. We should reject in the process those badly worn stereotypes that some persons still relish.

THE EVANGELICAL

We derive the term "evangelical" from *evangelion* ("evangel," "gospel," or "good news"). "Now I make known to you, brethren, the gospel which I preached to you, which also you received, in which also you stand," Paul elaborates, "that Christ died for our sins according to the Scriptures, and that He was buried, and that He was raised on the third day according to the Scriptures" (I Cor. 15:1,3–4). The apostle thus described the gospel in terms of the death-resurrection of Jesus.

Some naturally wonder how such an emphasis would distinguish the evangelical from other professing Christians. Karl Barth answers that the term "evangelical" means "informed by the gospel of Jesus Christ, as heard afresh in the sixteenth-century Reformation by direct return to Holy Scripture."[2] The Reformation qualifies as an evangelical event because it provided renewed emphasis on the gospel as critical for all of life.

The evangelical vigorously declares the death-resurrection of Jesus as God's solution to man's dilemma, and thereby treats other theological concerns as of secondary importance. When interested in liturgy, he treats it as a complementary concern; when involved in social action, he considers it an outgrowth of the gospel; when stressing the gifts of the Spirit, he means to adorn the good news. The evangelical views the gospel as critical for every additional consideration.

The evangelical option also implies a loyalty to Scripture. It resists the temptation to substitute some novel alternative to the Biblical interpretation of the person, work, and teaching of the Lord. It means to take Scripture seriously, to accept the Scriptural portrait rather than manufacture something more acceptable to the contemporary mood.

The most obvious illustration of tampering with Biblical revelation concerns those who take a second source of authority as normative. A less evident example is when an individual or a group claims privileged insight unavailable to others. An even more subtle instance involves carrying some legitimate interest to the point of twisting the meaning of Scripture.

The mark of a true evangelical is the evangelical's advocacy of the gospel as set forth in the Scriptures. The evangelical allows any number of related interests so long as they remain subsidiary to the good news and do not threaten the primacy of Holy Writ in defining the character of faith and practice.

A RESPONSE TO THE ENLIGHTENMENT

Some persons prefer to trace the modern evangelical movement from the Reformation, as might be implied from the quotation cited from Karl Barth. There may be merit in doing so, but we would have to qualify the claim with care. In the first place, we have seen that the evangelical principle derives from Scripture itself and not from some subsequent historical event. The Reformation was not exclusively nor solely an evangelical revival, no matter how large a part the evangelical concern may have played in it.

In the second place, there have been evangelical stirrings before and since the Reformation.[3] (The Roman Catholic of evangelical leaning has little difficulty citing precedents apart from the Reformers.)

The modifier "modern" allows us an easier point of reference in our quest for the origin of contemporary evangelicalism. The Enlightenment has been described as "the age which brought together the humanistic spirit of the Renaissance and the scientific revolution of the seventeenth century and thereby ushered in what we call 'the modern world.' "[4] We may therefore think of the modern evangelical movement as a response to the Enlightenment and a persisting commitment to the gospel according to the Scriptures.

The Enlightenment found it too easy to overlook its indebtedness to Christian doctrine, choosing rather to think of itself as a secular crusade against religious domination. Its advocates "were right to think of themselves as modern, secular philosophers, wrong to claim that they owed Christian culture nothing."[5] Thus the modern era began with a warped understanding of its Christian past and failed to take advantage of its legacy.

The reactions to the Enlightenment were varied. Some took to the secular course, intent on this life and what values we may realize here and now. This seed thought subsequently grew into the atheistic social philosophy of Karl Marx. Others allowed for a natural religion, in contrast to a revealed faith, asserting their belief in a Supreme Being, immortality, and the good life.

Friedrich Schleiermacher, in the vanguard of much of nineteenth-century theology, described religion as "an affection, a revelation of the Infinite and the finite."[6] He intended to salvage religion from the discard heap to which the Enlightenment had relegated it, but the result was a generally diluted Christianity, largely stripped of its historic convictions.[7]

No Watered-down Gospel

The evangelical spirit was not so disposed; it could not settle for a watered-down gospel. The evangelical concern contributed to Protestant fundamentalism in the conflict with modernism. It was not, strictly speaking, identical with fundamentalism (whose major characteristic was to support a pre-Enlightenment synthesis of Christianity and culture) but often an impetus, colleague, and defender.

We pick up the trail of the modern evangelical movement with the modernist's appraisal of the issue: the fundamentalist's "essential characteristic is a mind closed to new truth. All alike, whether Catholic Fundamentalist or Protestant Fundamentalist, believe that in a particular period in the past the full revelation of truth was completed. If Protestant Fundamentalist, the period of completion will perhaps be the seventeenth century; if 'Catholic' Fundamentalist, it will be the thirteenth."[8] It is interesting to note that the modernists saw fundamentalism as clinging to archaic traditions rather than defending the Scriptures.

It follows, as the modernists viewed the matter, that they themselves were the true disciples of Jesus. They alone adhered to the dynamic, ongoing course of revelation. They advocated the spirit and not the letter of the word.

Thereby the modernists meant to minister to contemporary man, as the Lord had done in his time. They were plagued by the fundamentalists, whom they thought of as the modern counterparts of the Jewish legalists.

What the modernist failed to appreciate was how deep a cleavage the Enlightenment had made between his understanding of the Christian faith and the understanding of those followers of Christ who preceded him. The modernist closed the book on seventeen centuries of conviction with hardly a twinge of conscience and then attempted to make peace with the contemporary era.

Nevertheless, the modernist's criticism of fundamentalism did not totally miss the mark. Fundamentalism, whether Protestant or Roman Catholic, tended to defend a position that had crystalized at a time subsequent to the writing of the Scriptures. It was inclined to equate Biblical commitment and a conservative preference,[9] and did at times fall prey to the very things with which the modernist categorically charged it.

GROWING SUPPORT

We are only a generation removed from the fundamentalist/modernist controversy and its effect lingers on. The issue of reconciling contemporary man to the claims of Christ is still very much the priority concern among evangelicals. The evangelical principle of taking the gospel as faithfully represented in Holy Writ holds steadfast and enjoys an astonishing ground swell of support. Much of this support comes from splinter movements (such as the Conservative Baptists), although joined by new efforts (as the Bible Baptists), ethnically conservative (General Conference Baptists), or an occasional old-line denomination (Southern Baptists). In the past few years the evangelical movement has also been spreading through the so-called old-line denominations (Presbyterian, Episcopal, Congregational, Roman Catholic), sometimes with a rapidity resembling a forest fire.

Even where the gains are less pronounced, a few zealous evangelicals may exert a great influence within their larger church fellowship. In one instance I was invited to speak from a pulpit previously guarded against the evangelical witness. The congregation's response to my simple exposition of Scripture was most favorable, but I puzzled over how the invitation had come about in the first place. Finally, after the service had terminated, a friendly couple introduced themselves. They had been busily engaged with the children's church, where they carried on a vigorous evangelical testimony. Then, during the interim between pastors, these folk persuaded the others to allow a representative of the evangelical faith to minister to them. This initial contact resulted in easing some of the prejudice previously fostered in that parish and provided support for the couple's efforts.

Such *dispersed* evangelicals tend to rely on radio and television broadcasts, literature, community Bible study, or the like, to contribute to their spiritual growth. They seldom find their needs adequately met in the local congregation and pursue the understanding of Scripture individually, as well as those responsibilities clarified in the process.

Dean Kelley's commentary on the varying fortunes of religious groups today seems especially pertinent as we focus on the contemporary evangelical movement. Kelley recognizes that

1. It is generally assumed that religious enterprises, if they want to succeed, will be reasonable, rational, courteous, responsible, restrained, and receptive to outside criticism; that is, they will want to preserve a good image in the world (as the world defines all these terms).

2. It is expected, moreover, that they will be democratic and gentle in their internal affairs (again, as the world defines these qualities).

3. They will also be responsive to the needs of men (as

currently conceived), and will want to work cooperatively with other groups to meet those needs.

4. They will not let dogmatism, judgmental moralism, or obsession with cultic purity stand in the way of such cooperation and service.[10]

"These expectations are a recipe," Kelley adds, not for the success but for "the failure of the religious enterprise."

Underscore the phrases "as the world defines these qualities" and "as currently conceived" and we discover the hallmark for both the Enlightenment and the general religious accommodation to it. Then, strip the description of its pejorative terminology and an evangelical could readily identify with the contrary point of view. He is less concerned with being *current* than *Christian*.

FIRST A CHRISTIAN

The evangelical is first and foremost a Christian. He takes no delight in being thought of as archaic, dogmatic, or unreasonable, but he refuses to let the world dictate his convictions. All of life for the evangelical hinges on the death-resurrection of Jesus Christ. He can substitute his own name for that of the apostle, when the latter announced: "Paul, a bond-servant of Christ Jesus, . . . set apart for the gospel of God, which He promised beforehand through His prophets in the holy Scriptures, concerning His Son, who was born of the seed of David according to the flesh, who was declared with power to be the Son of God by the resurrection from the dead, according to the Spirit of holiness, Jesus Christ our Lord" (Rom. 1:1–4). In spite of the protests of the self-styled liberated person, the evangelical finds such faith more stable than the convictions that change from generation to generation.

"The gospel of God" through "the holy Scriptures" sets forth the evangelical agenda. Here the evangelicals stand, God helping them, they can do no other. Often misunderstood, sometimes ridiculed, the evangelical does not claim omniscence, but affirms, "I know whom I have believed and I am convinced that He is able to guard what I have entrusted to Him until that day" (II Tim. 1:12). To do less would be to deny the Lord and that is the last thing the evangelical wants to do.

READER'S SUMMARY

We shall sum up this purposefully brief introduction to the evangelical resurgence:

1. We have become aware of a substantial evangelical awakening around the world. This is of such magnitude that it may easily become recognized as the most significant religious development of our time. But even if such an evaluation is too extravagant, the contemporary evangelical movement deserves a much more serious consideration than we have generally given it.

2. The evangelical claims the redeeming work of Christ as the core of his faith. His varied interests remain secondary to the proclamation of the gospel: "All these things are from God, who reconciled us to Himself through Christ, and gave us the ministry of reconciliation" (II Cor. 5:18).

3. The evangelical takes the Scripture as normative for our understanding of the person and work of Christ. He judges that we handle timeless truth and that no subsequent development should substantially affect its abiding message. He must remind himself as well as others that these words will be brought in judgment against us when the opinions of man have been forgotten.

4. The evangelical reasserts his confidence in the gospel

as a contemporary testimony. He does not mean to ignore the modern era but neither does he mean to accept its views uncritically.

5. This helps us to appreciate the nature of the fundamentalist/modernist controversy, the former in defense of the fundamentals of the Christian faith and the latter as regards the integrity of modern man. We saw that the modernist viewed his antagonist as bound to a previous century but failed to realize the extent of his own alienation from the historic gospel. His barbs did not totally miss the target but failed to hit dead center.

6. The evangelical movement is an alternative to our easy accommodation to the Enlightenment but nevertheless purposes to speak to contemporary man. The evangelical acknowledges that a prior application of the gospel to culture (whether in the seventeenth or the thirteenth century) will not suffice for today but he refuses to use this fact as an excuse for compromising the gospel.

Part

I

IN DEFENSE OF ORTHODOXY

was laid because some heresy had arisen which threatened to change the nature of Christianity and to destroy its central faith."[3] The cause of Christian orthodoxy was carried out on the firing line where conflicting claims competed for the allegiance of men. For all of the reflection required, it was not the result of meditating within some protected cloister.

The most serious of the early threats to orthodox Christianity came from Gnosticism. Gnosticism intended to work out a compatible compromise between Christianity and some current religious ideas. For instance, Gnosticism held that the world was divided between the good and evil powers, identifying spirit with the good and matter with evil. For this reason, Gnosticism repudiated the thought of God as the creator and held out the hope that the soul might be delivered through secret knowledge and the denial of the flesh. It also fostered the notion that Christ was sent by God to free men from the chains of matter, while rejecting that God truly became man in the process.

Christian orthodoxy rose to contend with this heresy, as it would with countless others down through the centuries. The Apostles' Creed, the most widely used of the Christian confessions, reflects this tension with Gnosticism. It asserts faith in "God, the Father Almighty, Maker of heaven and earth" as a repudiation of the Gnostic position that the created world is evil per se. It also states belief in "Jesus Christ His only Son, our Lord; who was conceived by the Holy Ghost, born of the Virgin Mary, suffered under Pontius Pilate, was crucified, dead, and buried" in contrast to the Gnostic's denial of Jesus' humanity. It places confidence as well in the "Holy Ghost, the Holy Catholic Church, the communion of saints, the forgiveness of sins, the resurrection of the body, the life everlasting" in conflict with the fundamental dualism of the Gnostics.

The Apostles' Creed not only illustrates the dynamic of Christian orthodoxy but also suggests the predictable line of thought it has pursued in other instances. No creed should be thought to express exactly or exclusively what the Bible teaches; rather, creeds set limits within which the orthodox Christian finds it proper to operate. The creed says this and not that, as if to steer us down a certain channel but not to prejudice what we discover along the way.

The Enlightenment initiated a confrontation with Christian orthodoxy. Not only did it pressure the church from without but it established an alliance with a growing number of adherents from within the fellowship. As a result, the orthodox Christian suffered relentless attack from all directions.

The evangelical faith defends the case for Christian orthodoxy.[4] It means to hold fast to the truth as previously delivered to the apostles and sustained by generations of those who continued in their doctrine. It undertakes this task as a personal obligation and example to others professing to be Christians.

The evangelical's commitment to orthodox Christianity suggests that we can derive from the Apostles' Creed (as a prime document of Christian orthodoxy) the main thrust of the evangelical faith. We can by reflecting on the Creed sense where the evangelical digs his trenches and maintains his line of fire.

God the Father

"I believe," we recall the words once more, "in God, the Father Almighty, Maker of heaven and earth." Gar-

diner Day comments: "If you were to have asked the
disciples what the Trinity meant, they would not have
known what you were talking about, for the word 'Trinity' is not mentioned in the New Testament. Had you
asked them about their experience of God in three Persons as Creator, as Jesus Christ, and as the Holy Spirit,
their eyes would have lighted and they would have no
difficulty in telling you about it. They knew the love of
God; they knew the grace of the Lord Jesus Christ; they
knew the fellowship of the Holy Spirit in their own experience."[5] They readily understood and could testify to the
truth expressed in Paul's benediction: "The grace of the
Lord Jesus Christ, and the love of God, and the fellowship of the Holy Spirit, be with you all" (II Cor. 13:14).

The Creed does not, strictly speaking, develop the
Trinitarian doctrine; it nowhere seeks to *explain* the
three-in-oneness of God. Rather, it is interested in de-
scribing how God relates to the world and where man
qualifies as the prime consideration.[6]

(The evangelical does not care to waste his time quib-
bling over terms, except as they have come to represent
important truths. He is sympathetic to any improvement
we can make on the creedal confessions but resists the
erosion of Biblical truth in the process of revising them.)

"For even if there are so-called gods whether in heaven
or on earth, as indeed there are many gods and many
lords," Paul deftly reasons, "yet for us there is but one
God, the Father, from whom are all things, and we exist
for Him; and one Lord, Jesus Christ, through whom are
all things, and we exist through Him" (I Cor. 8:5–6). The
apostle clearly intends to contrast belief in "the Father"
to the pagan pantheon and belief in the "one Lord" to
all conflicting allegiances—as if to repudiate theoretical
polytheism on the one hand and practical polytheism on

the other. Paul indicates that we should set aside the false gods we profess or those we unwittingly serve.

The Creed acted as an uncompromising attack on the popular practice of religious syncretism in the Roman Empire. It required converts to leave all competing deities in order to embrace the Almighty. Clean out the household gods, be done with the mystery religions, reject the worship of the emperor, and covenant with the living God.

While belief in the pantheon weakened before the advance of Christianity, conflicting loyalties remained:

There is practical polytheism not only in the worship of diverse material things, when men make money or pleasure or any other secular good the object of their idolatry, but also in all multiplication of "absolute" values as standing in their own right and deserving independent pursuit. It is possible, for example, to think of Truth, Beauty, and Goodness in this way. No such value can for the Christian be absolute in the strict sense of the word. There are many good things, but all are subordinate, relative—in St. Augustine's phrase, to be "referred" to God who is their Source. Nothing but the One God is to be worshipped.[7]

So we see practical polytheism on two levels, the rather crude preference for creature comforts and the more cultured appeal to the True, the Beautiful, and the Good.

One of the earliest examples of evangelical humor that stays with me had to do with a convert reluctant to get his wallet wet during Baptism. With a none-too-subtle play on words, the point was that for us to escape idolatry Jesus must be Lord over our material possessions.

The cultured polytheist seems to find it easier to escape the preacher's notice. He tacks "to the glory of God" on the end of his obsession with philosophy, art, or the ethical life and everyone applauds his performance. But truth for its own sake can be a misleading maxim, as also with beauty or goodness. They offer liberty but in time enslave us to some abstract notion or passing fancy. It is better, as the Creed views life, to pursue the God of truth, beauty, and goodness, for in and through him we come to appreciate all else of worth.

The other feature of the orthodox disenchantment with polytheism is the lapse of God's personal characteristics. He appears as the "ground of being," or some equally obscure reference, rather than as the living God of Abraham, Isaac, and Jacob. He is the incomprehensible force instead of the Father of our Lord, Jesus Christ.

The evangelical reasons otherwise. He assumes that God would address man in an intelligible tongue and take pleasure in doing so. This fact does not diminish God's greatness in the least; rather, it accents his love for us.

"When we confess our belief in one God the Father," Burnaby summarizes quickly, "we are confessing our belief that God who sent his only-begotten Son to redeem us has thereby given to believers the right to call themselves God's children, to pray and to live as Christ prayed and lived."[8] The creedal conviction comes both harder and easier than the popular expression concerning God as the Father. It does not hold with the view that the paternal nature is immediately evident in the affairs of men. The fortunes of life are generally ambiguous at this point; one person escapes an accident in which another dies.

We learn of the Father through Jesus' life and ministry, through his obedience and sense of communion. "He has not left Me alone," Jesus confided, "for I always do the things that are pleasing to Him" (John 8:29)—as one would observe the wishes of the head of the family and enjoy his commendation.

Jesus' listeners prided themselves on being sons of Abraham and children of God, but the Master told them plainly that they were of their father the devil, and wanted to do the desires of their father (John 8:44). Like father, like son.

Jesus' life-style stood in sharp contrast to theirs. They courted death, he life; they lied, he told the truth. Perhaps all persons do not show their evil so readily, the evangelical imagines, but the credibility gap increases whenever we turn aside from the Christ to look at others or the events through which we pass. We learn to think of God as the Father, not as a presumptive step but in the role of a disciple of Christ.

The road of discipleship inevitably brings us into lively interaction with *sinners.* [9] We sit with Jesus as he ate with those irreligious persons, his purpose being to demonstrate the Father's concern for prodigals and to elicit a response from them. The prodigal in Jesus' parable admitted that he had revolted against heaven and in God's sight, and had forfeited his right as a son. But the father ordered the best robe brought forth and put upon him, a ring put on his hand and sandals on his feet, and the fattened calf prepared for a time of festivity (Luke 15: 21–24). Sinners, like the prodigal, may enjoy the fellowship of God, having retraced those difficult steps homeward to the waiting Father. This story suggests something of the pleasure that evangelicals associate with conversion.

THE ALMIGHTY

"If God were good, he should want to make his creatures happy," the common charge runs. "If he were capable, he could do so: seeing we do not always experience felicity, God must not be good, capable, or both." The evangelical has generally selected one of two lines of response, one touching upon man's volitional nature and the other with the purpose for which God intended him.

Man is a free moral agent (not an automaton, or robot, or similar mechanical device). With such freedom comes the possibility of bad choice as well as good, and bad consequences as well as the better ones. On the positive side of the ledger, man enjoys the rewards derived from a course of action wisely selected, persevered in, and shared with others. The whole creative interplay of persons is a plus factor to the exercise of free will, an orchestration of life.

It does no good to argue solely from the negative considerations of the case. The credits and debits must be entered once the ledger is opened for business.

One can read volumes on the preceding sketch, but we turn instead to the purpose for which man was created. When God neared the end of his creative activity, he determined to make man in his own image and to have communion with him.

Why should we suppose that God would stop short of achieving the goal set for man, especially in the light of his declared might and steadfast compassion? We can only appreciate the notion of God Almighty in connection with his implementing such a high calling for man.

Of course, the term "Almighty" does not precisely imply what those had in mind who formulated the problem concerning the divine omnipotence which allows human suffering. It means to convey the strength of God in contrast to human weakness, and at that point there can be little question.

"Hallelujah!" rolls the voice of a great multitude. "For the Lord our God, the Almighty, reigns" (Rev. 19:6). Here we discover the significance of the Creed's confidence, in the sovereignty of God over the affairs of men. God manages to bring good out of even the most difficult aspects of life and reckons with evil in the process.

MAKER OF HEAVEN AND EARTH

The Creed encourages us to think of the sovereign God as the creator and sustainer of life, like the child who prays around the objects he sees in the room. "Thank you, God, for the desk," his eyes traveling from one subject to another. "Thank you, God, for the chairs, the red one and the green one." It urges us to consider that "apart from Him nothing came into being that has come into being" (John 1:3).

The evangelical reasons that there was purpose in our origin, that there is purpose in our experience at this moment and in the promise of the future. There are only two explanations for life, when reduced to the simplest options: chance and providence. To bolster the argument for what amounts to a chance-based universe, one may refine matters so as to argue that purpose originated later, with man or at some other point. (The analogy would be that of a person who decides to gamble on the roll of dice.) But this is nothing more than a refinement and may obscure the basic alternatives.

J. Edwin Orr likes to tell about the time when he was walking along a beach and found the sand scooped out to resemble first one continent and then another. He refused to believe that some enterprising crab had done this and soon came across a youngster with shovel in hand, the creative designer of those representations he had previously seen. Chance and providence remain the alternative explanations for the origin and preservation of life.

Orr proceeds, in characteristic evangelical fashion, to

press the preference for a purpose option. "A Christian believes that the complex design of the universe is a result of the planning of a Super-Intelligence. This is most reasonable. If you can show me that it is unreasonable, or that any other explanation is more reasonable, I shall withdraw the argument."[10] Of course, we must bear in mind that Orr views life over Jesus' shoulder and that strengthens one's confidence considerably.

What are the implications of this perspective? That God created well. Nothing is evil by nature, according to the Creed. "For St. Paul, the things that are seen are temporal and the things that are not seen are eternal; but St. Paul would never have said that the things that are seen are evil because they are temporal. It follows that it cannot be the aim of the human spirit to escape from the body by flight, through contempt of the 'flesh.' The way of union with God is not by any attempt to shake off the conditions of our bodily nature."[11] This point of view also forbids that we see anything evil in the limitations of finiteness. It is not our finiteness as such but our pride in the face of it that leads to sin.

A good creation testifies to its Benefactor. "He did not leave Himself without witness," Paul concluded, "in that He did good and gave you rains from heaven and fruitful seasons, satisfying your hearts with food and gladness" (Acts 14:17). The apostle knew full well that life is by no means without its blemishes. It is, rather, by God's triumph over evil that we can judge that the rains from heaven are but the earnest of the refreshing yet to come.

The Scriptures teach, the Creed affirms, and the evangelical believes that God acts toward man as the sovereign Father, creator and sustainer of life. It is not an easily assumed faith and rather presumptive apart from Jesus' tutoring. Yet the assurance builds as we walk the road to discipleship, forsaking all else to accompany the Lord.

READER'S SUMMARY

Now we pause to look over the ground recently covered:

1. The evangelical movement is set in defense of Christian orthodoxy. It never meant to create something new, but to commend the traditional faith as it was expressed through the centuries. It intended to depart only as appropriate to address the most recent heresies growing out of the Enlightenment.

2. We were able to turn to the Apostles' Creed, as a primary document of orthodox Christianity, in order to extend our understanding of the evangelical persuasion. Thus we recognize that "they know the love of God; they know the grace of the Lord Jesus Christ; they know the fellowship of the Holy Spirit in their own experience." They bear witness to a persisting relationship rather than contend over some abstract dogma.

3. We centered on that portion of the Creed which expresses faith "in God, the Father Almighty, Maker of heaven and earth." The evangelical acknowledges the love of God. "Just as a father has compassion on his children," the psalmist enthused, "so the Lord has compassion on those who fear Him" (Ps. 103:13).

4. The evangelical likewise holds that God can turn every eventuality to eternal gain. He perceives of the Almighty as delivering him *in* rather than *from* the difficult circumstances of life. Nothing seems too hard for God when appreciated in such a setting.

5. It follows that we should view life purposefully. We should see in our origin a gracious design and in our

experience enduring significance. Life is essentially good, for all of its distress and agony. Much as Job reflected: "Shall we indeed accept good from God and not accept adversity?" (Job 2:10). Not that such an opinion can be cultivated readily, but it grows as we follow in the Master's footsteps.

3

Witness to Jesus Christ

Between the Creed's affirmation of belief in God the
Father and in Jesus Christ the evangelical pauses only
long enough to catch his breath. The two stand together,
each contributing to the other, alike confessions of how
the Christian sees God at work. They are planks in the
platform of Christian orthodoxy and therefore of central
importance to evangelical thinking.

JESUS CHRIST

The words "Jesus Christ" have become so thought-
lessly fused as to sound like a person's given and family
names. Left behind are the denials, uncertainties, and
indecision of those contemporaries of Jesus who wondered whether he was the Christ, as may also be the
confidence that some of them gained in the process.

Jesus of Nazareth as the promised Messiah is abridged
to these two words in the Creed, "Jesus Christ." Not
even the article remains, not Jesus *the* Christ but Jesus
Christ, so tightly does faith draw this critical assertion in
the Creed.

In order to appreciate the evangelical's stance, we shall
have to separate the historical figure from his office, and
dwell on the quest of the historical Jesus. "Protestant

Orthodoxy had the effect, in its theology and writings, of harmonizing all the biblical accounts into one smooth composite. . . . The first real change in the study of the life of Jesus, one which removed such study from the protective cover of Christian piety, came with the rise of rationalism and critical Bible study in the eighteenth century."[1] The latter rode in on the tide of the Enlightenment.

The tendency in Christian orthodoxy, whether second century or seventeenth century, was to harmonize Scripture into one uniform portrait of Jesus. The evangelical mood, the later opposition notwithstanding, has been similarly inclined. It assumes that the New Testament gives a credible testimony as to the person, life, and teaching of Jesus.

The nineteenth-century rash of biographies of Jesus predictably combined a theological skepticism with a historical naïveté. The former led the authors to take issue with the New Testament text; the latter permitted them to draw unwarranted alternatives. It was a venture destined to produce an endless variety of *jesuses*, to satisfy the prejudices of the biographers and their readers.

Albert Schweitzer's *The Quest of the Historical Jesus* called an end to the "old quest" for the historical Jesus and anticipated the next development. "It was no small matter, therefore, that the course of the critical study of the life of Jesus, after a resistance lasting for two generations, during which first one expediency was tried and then another, theology was forced by genuine history to begin to doubt the artificial history with which it had thought to give new life to our Christianity." Schweitzer set aside the former effort to speculate along another line. "But the truth is, it is not Jesus as historically known, but Jesus as spiritually arisen within man, who is significant for our time and can help it."[2]

Schweitzer's protest led us away from the quest of the historical Jesus to a proclamation of the Christ of faith. The old lives of Jesus might as well burn, Rudolf Bultmann concluded, since our concern is with the exalted Lord.

This shift of direction soon ran its course as well. "Finally the pendulum has swung a third time, not back to the extremes of the 19th-century Quest, but at least away from the 'no biography' extreme, back toward the center and toward some interest in the Jesus of history."[3] It was a chastised return to the Jesus of history but a return nonetheless.

The evangelical has stood a bit to the side of these vigorous swings of the pendulum, holding first to a presumed better understanding of Jesus than had the early disciples, to professed disinterest, and to a restrained investigation of the sources, relatively little moved in his confidence in Holy Writ. Not unaware of the frantic changes in direction, he holds a more settled course for himself. The evangelical, in defense of Christian orthodoxy, is inclined to harmonize the Biblical records and count the difficulties in doing so as rather minor considerations to the overall enterprise. He confesses "Jesus Christ" as the historical Jesus who fulfilled the Messianic promise; the person and office combined, merged in time and for eternity.

HIS ONLY SON, OUR LORD

The orthodox Creed continues as if to clarify what has been said or perhaps extend it. The construction suggests that the ideas of Jesus' being Son and Lord must be closely related, perhaps not as indivisibly as with "Jesus

Christ" but more like opposite sides of the identical coin.

This added phrase implies two relationships, one to the Father and the other to the disciples. It is as though Jesus were stationed between the two in a mediating position, as indeed was the intent.

To talk of Jesus as "His only Son" amounts to placing an exclamation mark after the personality of God. He is really personal, his mystery notwithstanding! The evangelical has been adamant at this point. He views the "unknown God" of ancient Athens as lacking in personal attributes, and the product of pagan rather than Christian thinking.

This perspective leads us to a related conviction. God acts in keeping with his revealed purposes. No swerving in one direction or another, no overreaction from which to recover, no backtracking from a false start. His activity, for all its variation, reflects a marvelous continuity from beginning to end, from the patriarchs, through the prophets, to his only Son.

The evangelical likewise lingers on the uniqueness of Jesus' relationship to the Father, not only in his regard for the Biblical teaching but also in reaction to the nineteenth-century claim for a spark of divinity in every man. "We do not yet see all things subjected to" man, "but we do see Him who has been made for a little while lower than the angels, namely, Jesus, because of the suffering of death crowned with glory and honor, that by the grace of God He might taste death for every one" (Heb. 2:8–9). There lies the contrast between fallen man and the faithful Christ. "There is one God," the evangelical often repeats the text, "and one mediator also between God and men, the man Christ Jesus" (I Tim. 2:5).

If Jesus is God's only Son, then he is rightfully our Lord. Jesus told a parable concerning a landowner who put his property in the hands of certain workers and took a journey (Matt. 21:33–46). When harvesttime arrived, he sent several of his servants to receive what was due him, only to have them beaten, stoned, or killed. The owner then sent a larger company of men to secure his property but had the same result. Thereupon, he determined to commission his son, supposing that "they will respect my son." Well they should, but instead they murdered the heir, meaning to keep the rich inheritance for themselves.

The application was all too obvious. Would you kill the Son and rightful beneficiary to all things? Jesus taught that "not every one who says to Me, 'Lord, Lord,' will enter the kingdom of heaven; but he who does the will of My Father who is in heaven" (Matt. 7:21). The doers of God's will, believe; and the believers, do. We revere the only Son by treating his wishes as our commands.

His Humiliation

"Who was conceived by the Holy Ghost, born of the Virgin Mary, suffered under Pontius Pilate; was crucified, dead, and buried; He descended into hell" reads the Creed by way of addressing what has come to be called the "humiliation of Christ." We may define the humiliation as the concern and consequent action by which Jesus forged his way fully into human life without compromise to sin.

The idea is most clearly expressed as the basis of Paul's appeal to the Philippian church: "Do nothing from selfishness or empty conceit, but with humility of mind let each of you regard one another as more important than himself; do not merely look out for your own personal interests, but also for the interests of others. Have this attitude in yourselves which was also in Christ Jesus, who, although He existed in the form of God, did not regard equality with God a thing to be grasped, but emptied Himself, taking the form of a bond-servant, and being made in the likeness of men. And being found in appearance as a man, He humbled Himself by becoming obedient to the point of death, even death on a cross" (Phil. 2:3–8). The Creed divides the preceding into three segments, which relate to Jesus' life, death, and descent into hell.

Birth and death are two poles between which life must travel. So the psalmist comments:

> As for the days of our life, they contain
>   seventy years,
> Or if due to strength, eighty years.
> Yet their pride is but labor and sorrow;
> For soon it is gone and we fly away.
>   (Ps. 90:10)

A span of years, extended in some instances for a brief time longer, and then gone. So quickly and imperceptibly does life pass that it seldom leaves an imprint on history.

Yet Jesus proved to be a remarkable exception. We read that he "was conceived by the Holy Ghost, born of the Virgin Mary." The Creed stresses both the humanity and the transcendent character of the Lord. John writes in a like vein, how "the Word became flesh, and dwelt among us, and we beheld His glory, glory as of the only begotten from the Father, full of grace and truth" (John 1:14). His flesh housed the Shekinah glory, the presence of God.

Persons have the unfortunate habit of making too much of either Christ's humanity or his deity, one at the expense of the other. Some stress his humanity so as to obscure, if not eliminate, any divine leverage on life. For any practical purposes, he becomes a well-meaning person, bequeathing ideals that the rest of us have difficulty implementing.

These persons should listen more attentively to the Creed as it solemnly intones "conceived by the Holy Ghost." This suggests "that the Incarnation was a totally *new* beginning in the world's story, in which the initiative lay solely with God. He came down from heaven; and that divine descent was into the weakness and fragility of human nature, not its strength. All that humanity, in Mary's person, could do was to accept the miracle of grace."[4] It was a miracle that casts all subsequent life within a new context, as the result of the divine visitation.

Others think of Christ in such an ethereal fashion as never to get his hands dirty. He flits through life, knowing all the answers before anyone can think up the questions. Some even disallowed that Jesus could die and proposed that God provided a stand-in for the occasion.

Such persons should observe the Creed where it adds "born of the Virgin Mary." Jesus never walked around with a halo hovering over his head to single him out from the rest. His feet touched the ground as he walked, his voice had no special resonance, his eyes no X-ray quality. Jesus was thoroughly human.

Birth stands out as a time of rejoicing, while suffering comes as an unwelcomed visitor. But there is in the course of life

> A time to weep, and a time to laugh;
> A time to mourn, and a time to dance.
> (Eccl. 3:4)

So Jesus experienced life in its varied forms, and commended it to us.

Jesus "suffered under Pontius Pilate." C. S. Lewis once proposed that four fifths of human pain is inflicted by other persons. "Ninety-nine percent" would be more accurate if we included the suffering that results from indifference.

The Buddhist and the Christian Scientist, to mention but two, try to purge pain at its source, but the orthodox Christian allows it room. While suffering is not desirable, he assesses it within the providential purpose of God. So Jesus approached life and set the course for others to follow.

The Master preferred life with all its demands to cutting corners. "When guilt, suffering, and death began their painful encirclement, he could have broken out, he could have spared all that humiliation just by a wave of his hand. Although it was possible for him to do it, that hand never moved. Instead, he let himself fall, living and dying, into the hands of his Father."[5] Jesus pressed ahead, where needs became overwhelming, the way threatening, the flesh weary. He lived life to its full.

Jesus forged on to confront the grim reaper. The cold nibbled at his fingertips, images lost their distinctiveness, voices faded into the distance, the night of death fell. Without exception the curtain drops on life's drama, but faith draws from Jesus the triumphant cry, "It is finished!" (John 19:30). It was the conclusion, not of life alone, but of service awaiting its recognition. Jesus had completed all that he had been called upon to do and was now content to abide by the "Well done, good and faithful slave; you were faithful with a few things, I will put you in charge of many things, enter into the joy of your master" (Matt. 25:21).

I am aware that Christianity draws criticism for its stress on dying *well*. The point is that we never really come to grips with life without facing the prospect of death. The person who crowds death out of his thinking can never get life into focus either. We live as stewards about to be asked to account for our activity. Blessed is the man who can make out his Shepherd's staff against the gathering dusk of death.

Jesus suffered not merely demise but "even death on the cross," as Paul accents the matter. That the Messiah should meet such an ignoble end appears to have been an issue for considerable controversy. "This Man, delivered up by the predetermined plan and foreknowledge of God," Peter argued, "you nailed to a cross by the hands of godless men and put Him to death" (Acts 2:23). Jesus was socially castigated but divinely approved.

Some have taken the descent to hell as simply reinforcing the fact of death, the experience of forsakenness in particular; others take it as a subsequent ministry to those who died in anticipation of God's messianic deliverance. In any case, "no matter how distant the region we penetrate with our thoughts, no matter how oppressive the desert—even hell and the kingdom of death, we always encounter the glory of Jesus, welcoming us and offering us security."[6] Jesus walked to the end of the road in order to minister to us each step of the way.

His Exaltation

The exaltation of Christ, as outlined in the Creed, consists of the resurrection, ascension, session, and second advent. Paul ties all these together in his correspondence with the awesome figure of a general who has engaged the enemy (the humiliation), breaks their resistance (the resurrection), enjoys the fruits of victory (the session), and stamps out the final opposition (the second advent).[7] He concludes with reference to Christ as equipping "the saints for the work of service, to the building up of the body of Christ" (Eph. 4:12).

Historic Christianity, as the evangelical appraises it, ceases to exist apart from the resurrection. Christian faith is resurrection faith. Drop the phrase "the third day He arose from the dead" and the Christian position topples like a house of cards. Paul testifies that Jesus "was declared with power to be the Son of God by the resurrection from the dead" (Rom. 1:4). John describes how Thomas refused to believe what the other disciples said concerning the risen Christ, until confronted himself, after which he cried out, "My Lord and my God!" (John 20:28). "Because you have seen Me, have you believed?" Jesus chided Thomas' reluctance. "Blessed are they who did not see, and yet believed" (v. 29).

The resurrection was treated as an empirical event, something evident to the senses, where one's finger could feel the nail print and the hand might follow the spear's thrust into Jesus' side. "See My hands and My feet, that it is I Myself," Jesus reassured them; "touch Me and see, for a spirit does not have flesh and bones as you see that I have" (Luke 24:39).

Some reject the idea of a bodily resurrection in favor of a less tangible alternative. They allow that a new spirit came upon the disciples, that *they* experienced a transformation, but this idea, taken by itself, would have set the early Christians to shaking their heads in protest. Had they not seen Jesus? Did he not invite them to touch his wounds? Had he not spoken with them?

This assurance of a bodily resurrection explains the importance the early church placed upon those who had been with Jesus during the time of his ministry and had become witnesses with them of His resurrection (Acts

1:22). The order of events was of a similar sort, available for men to see and report to others, whether an incident during Jesus' labors or his triumph over the grave.

The resurrection swept away any uncertainty as to Jesus' credibility. He "was declared with power to be the Son of God by the resurrection from the dead" (Rom. 1:4). This event acted as the confirmation to Jesus' prior claim.

The resurrection was also the crucial juncture in Christ's conquest of sin. Up to that point he contended with forces of evil, but the resurrection put them to flight. From there on, righteousness has the unalterable advantage of high ground from which to press its attack.

"No one has ascended into heaven," John quotes Jesus as saying, "but He who descended from heaven, even the Son of Man" (John 3:13). One cannot help pausing with this comment. No man has ascended but him whose proper place is heaven. Not even the prophets could make such a claim, only the individual whom John describes as the preexisting Word.

The term "Son of Man" strengthens the identity of this ascending one. "For just as the lightning comes from the east, and flashes even to the west, so shall the coming of the Son of Man be. . . . And they will see the Son of Man coming on the clouds of the sky with power and great glory." (Matt. 24:27, 30.)

The significance of Jesus' descending/ascending is that he provides our access to God. He is God's initiative toward man and man's avenue for return. He is the divinely constructed bridge.

"This hope we have as an anchor of the soul, a hope both sure and steadfast and one which enters within the veil, where Jesus has entered as a forerunner for us" (Heb. 6:19–20). Only the imagery has changed; the idea of Jesus as mediator remains constant. He has not only parted but *rent* the veil so that we might come boldly to the throne of grace. He passed through, that we might follow on his heels.

The critics may misunderstand the evangelical assurance generated by resurrection faith. "One unappreciated observer put it this way: 'They act as if they had God in their hip pocket.' "[8] He thought the evangelicals irreverent for the bold confidence they express for having "an anchor within the veil."

But if the ascension fans hope for the believer, the evangelical thinks it should strike fear in others: in those who declared their opposition and nailed Jesus to a cross; those who stood at a disinterested distance; those who pushed the whole matter out of their heads. Jesus warned of storm clouds gathering, apostasy and tribulation, men losing their direction in their haste to find shelter. Blessed is the man whose hope is in the Lord.

The Creed next describes Jesus as sitting "at the right hand of God the Father Almighty," there to administer God's rich provision for our service:

> O to grace how great a debtor
> Daily I'm constrained to be!
> Let Thy goodness like a fetter
> Bind my wandering heart to Thee.

For never a moment does the disciple go unattended; on no occasion does he labor alone. Grace, like a vigorous mountain stream, frolics into otherwise barren lives, to refresh, renew, and sustain.

Sensing Christ's session, we respond by devoting ourselves to his service.[9] We feel constrained to please him; even when contrary thoughts come to mind, we pray for strength to continue. "Let Thy goodness like a fetter bind my wandering heart to Thee."

There remains, so far as Christ's exaltation is concerned, the "blessed hope." Now, hope resembles faith cast into the future. It is not opting for some unrealistic fantasy but for confidence that what appears under way will reach a likely consummation. Hope, then, is less than sight but not even in league with credulity.

To use a World War II analogy, the Creed views Jesus' first advent as D-Day and his second advent as V-Day. The invasion of sin-dominated earth has been accomplished and there is no casting out of the Lord's regiments. The final pockets of resistance nevertheless persist, drawing upon every desperate strategy to fly in the face of eventual and utter defeat.

The Creed puts the consummation simply: "from thence He shall come to judge the quick and the dead." Here are none of the refinements that have often characterized more recent debate but a forthright statement, the more electrifying for its precision.

The second advent is a personal return. "This Jesus," the disciples were told, this identical figure, will come again (Acts 1:11). This gives rise to a personal hope, not primarily in some*thing* but for Some*one.* It is a sort of continuation of what the disciples had come to expect these several years: ever-new experiences as mediated by the always-faithful Lord.

It will likewise be an empirical event. It will occur "in just the same way as you have watched Him go into heaven" (Acts 1:11). "Every eye will see Him" (Rev. 1:7). Do not believe those who claim Christ to have come secretively among us, "for just as the lightning comes from the east, and flashes even to the west, so shall the coming of the Son of Man be" (Matt. 24:27).

It will also be a sovereign return. He shall "rule all the

nations with a rod of iron" (Rev. 12:5). The kingdoms of this world will "become the kingdom of our Lord, and of His Christ" (Rev. 11:15).

It is finally an imminent event. "Be on the alert then," Jesus warned, "for you do not know the day nor the hour" (Matt. 25:13). The uncertainty of the time was to provide our motivation for diligent stewardship. "Every one who has this hope fixed on Him," John extends the theme, "purifies himself, just as He is pure" (I John 3:3).

"This Jesus, who has been taken up from you into heaven," we now quote the text in full, "will come in just the same way as you have watched Him go into heaven." "This Jesus," a personal return; "in just the same way," a visible return; the disciples had inquired into the setting up of the kingdom, a sovereign return; to which Jesus replies that "it is not for you to know times or epochs which the Father has fixed by His own authority," an imminent return. Thus Christ's exaltation closes with the blessed hope, with faith pointed toward the future.

"God was in Christ," the Creed concurs, "reconciling the world to Himself" (II Cor. 5:19). He is like an aggressive general who carries the conflict to the enemy, brings it to a decisive victory, and shares the spoils of battle, in anticipation of an unconditional surrender. The evangelical finds these sentiments faithful to the teaching of Scripture, compatible with his experience, and constant with the testimony of orthodox Christianity.

READER'S SUMMARY

We now provide a general summary:

1. The Creed continues from its confession concerning God the Father to Jesus Christ. They are alike "planks in the platform of Christian orthodoxy and therefore of

central importance to evangelical thinking."

2. The union of the words "Jesus Christ" suggests that the historical figure of Jesus is indeed the expected Messiah. The evangelical has taken a dour attitude toward the efforts to distinguish between the Jesus of history and the Christ of faith, as if we could divorce what the early church saw as indivisible. One may accept or reject the significance of Jesus as represented in the New Testament, but fails in the attempt to get behind these records to discover a more authentic figure.

3. The evangelical also stresses the uniqueness of Jesus as the peculiar Son of God. He objects to the idea that there is "a spark of divinity in every man," as though Jesus were simply an elder brother.

4. "If Jesus is God's only Son, then he is rightfully our Lord." So the evangelical understands the Biblical rationale for the confession that Jesus is Lord!

5. The Creed stresses the advent of Christ by way of an invading general who engages the enemy, presses the initial confrontation, strikes the critical blow, leads the vanquished in triumphant display, and eventually puts down the remaining resistance. The first aspect of this struggle has been called the humiliation, "the concern and consequent action by which Jesus forged his way fully into human life without compromise to sin." For the evangelical, the humiliation implies that he should not hold back from the demands that life makes upon him. He intends vigorously to negotiate life as God gives him the grace to do so.

6. The exaltation, as the remaining element in Christ's ministry, describes how Christ effectively subjects all of life to the sovereign will of God. The Creed revels in the triumph of the resurrection, the Lord as now sustaining his loyal followers, and his imminent return. Thus we can

think of D-Day as an analogy for Jesus' first advent and V-Day for his second advent. Thus the evangelical rejoices in the conquest already achieved and its prospect for being consummated.

4

Accent on the Holy Spirit

The Creed expresses belief in the Holy Ghost without any further descriptive remarks. This is followed by a series of related affirmations bearing on the work of the Holy Spirit. These refer to the holy catholic church, the communion of saints, the forgiveness of sins, the resurrection of the body, and the life everlasting.

"The wind blows where it wishes and you hear the sound of it, but do not know where it comes from and where it is going," Jesus observed; "so is every one who is born of the Spirit" (John 3:8). Like the uncertain breeze that seems to spring up for no reason at all only to die down as quickly or turn direction at some whim or afterthought, the Holy Spirit behaves as if too shy to make a personal appearance but capable of such power as to make the mountains quake. The Spirit resembles a reluctant giant in our midst, unseen but testified to by his mighty works.

THE HOLY GHOST

John recalls the Master's promise: "I will ask the Father, and He will give you another Helper, that He may be with you forever; that is the Spirit of truth, whom the world cannot receive, because it does not behold Him or know Him, but you know Him because He abides with you, and will be in you" (John 14:16–17). As the Paraclete (one called alongside to assist), the Holy Spirit was not an utter stranger to the disciples but would assume a more intimate relationship with them.

Jesus' audience would have understood the reference to the Holy Spirit in connection with bringing life and order out of void and chaos. "The earth was formless and void, and darkness was over the surface of the deep" (Gen. 1:2). The world waited, sluggish and empty, until the Spirit worked so as to solicit the appreciative response of the psalmist:

> O Lord, how many are Thy works!
> In wisdom Thou hast made them all;
> The earth is full of Thy possessions.
> There is the sea, great and broad,
> In which are swarms without number,
> Animals both small and great.
> There the ships move along,
> And Leviathan, which Thou hast formed
> 　　　to sport in it.
> 　　　　　　　　　　(Ps. 104:24–26)

We can better grasp the ministry of the Spirit against the background of our own tenuous existence. "If we ascend only fifteen miles above our allotted territory, our blood begins to boil, and we perish," Thielicke observes. "Likewise, if we descend fifteen miles into the earth our life's thread is burned up. . . . The Creator has allotted us only a very thin band between the zones of death above and below. Here he reserves a space for us men to live in, and he holds back the threatening elements of destruction at its borders."[1] Woe to us, Thielicke concludes, should the creation "be reversed and the primal chaos break in."

Thus should we understand the complaint that "My Spirit shall not strive with man forever" (Gen. 6:3), as if to set a limit on the time he will hold at bay the forces so destructive to life. The great flood was a case in point, where the firmaments above and below converged on fragile humanity.

Jesus differentiated between what the world knew of the Holy Spirit and what was common knowledge for the disciples. The world "does not behold Him or know Him, but you know Him because He abides with you." The distinction appears to be rooted in the Hebrew legacy of the disciples and may have been improved upon from Jesus' instruction. They enjoyed a privileged insight into the work of the Spirit and assurance concerning it.

However, the coming of the Messiah had introduced a new phase of the Spirit's activity. Burnaby labels this the "synoptic silence" in that Jesus is pushed to the foreground.[2] The Holy Spirit is not less active than previously was the case but less obvious for reason of calling our attention to the Lord.

This Messianic turn in the Holy Spirit's ministry extended to the disciples as well. Whereas the Spirit had been *with* the disciples, the Spirit now would be *in* them. Jesus promised, "He will teach you all things, and bring to your remembrance all that I said to you" (John 14:26). The emphasis was still upon Jesus, and with this the community he brought into being.

Paul notes how "the Spirit also helps our weakness; for we do not know how to pray as we should, but the Spirit Himself intercedes for us with groanings too deep for words; and He who searches the hearts knows what the mind of the Spirit is, because He intercedes for the saints according to the will of God" (Rom. 8:26–27). "God alone knows what is in God, only his own Spirit knows the depths of his divinity."[3] Like understands like and man in his natural state is hindered in knowing God. He cannot and does not want to know God's will for his life. Here the Spirit assumes his ultimate role as the Paraclete who, knowing the way of God, supports man in that path.

Jesus prays for such Spirit-infused disciples. "I do not ask Thee to take them out of the world, but to keep them from the evil one" (John 17:15). Seeing they are no longer of the world, sustain life in them against the chaotic forces that threaten it, keep them from the evil powers of the world, and continue the good work already begun until I come again.[4]

The petition continues: "Sanctify them in the truth; Thy word is truth" (v. 17). Where the earlier request was negative ("Keep them from the evil one"), the latter is positive ("Sanctify them"). Sanctification, as we observe it at work in Jesus' life, meant involvement in the world but not enslavement to it. From that the disciple takes his cue and makes a commitment to life lived in the Spirit.

The petition persists: "That they may be one, just as We are one; I in them, and Thou in Me, that they may be perfected in unity" (vs. 22–23). Jesus did not advocate uniformity but a spirit of mutual consideration, where persons of dissimilar disposition and interests choose to work together for the benefit of all—an assembly where love reigns over every temptation to faction and competition.

The Spirit richly endows the Christian community with the means of satisfying Jesus' petition. He provides gifts, then ministries and effects.

The Holy Spirit bestows a priceless assortment of gifts on the church, individual gifts only insofar as seen as benefiting all. Gifts provide no excuse to boast or employ for selfish gain, but are a means for serving others.

The Holy Spirit also channels these gifts into the appropriate ministries to serve the Lord and others in his name. Paul can therefore confess, "There are varieties of ministries, and the same Lord" (I Cor. 12:5). The ministries all work together as outlets for the gifts and to benefit the entire community.

Gifts and ministries combine to achieve the desired results. With a word of comfort here, a rebuke there, the Holy Spirit creatively applies the resources at hand. He relates to unique individuals in their peculiar circumstances so as to further Jesus' call to community.

The petition concludes with Jesus' wish "that they also, whom Thou hast given Me, be with Me where I am, in order that they may behold My glory" (John 17:24). The beautific vision of Jesus as the Son is in one sense attested to by the indwelling Spirit but in another ever flirting with us until we see Jesus face to face in his glory. The present ministry of the Spirit builds an anticipation for a climax waiting in the future.

To believe in the Holy Spirit is to affirm that what Jesus desired is in the process of being achieved. It implies the restless labor of the Spirit to bring life out of the void, order out of chaos, glory out of despair. The Paraclete stands alongside to help, to lift up the fallen, console the sorrowing, heal the broken. Such has orthodox Christianity held, and the evangelical testifies to its truthfulness.

THE CHURCH

"The Church, the Communion of Saints, the Forgiveness of sins, the Resurrection of the body, and the Life Everlasting are all the result of God's creative action through the Holy Spirit."[5] Any discussion of the work of the Spirit flows naturally out into the remaining elements of the Creed.

The ministry of the Spirit takes on, of necessity, a

corporate nature, for Christians never exist as isolated
individuals. "The Church is the community of called-out-
ones, Abraham being its prototype and Israel its pattern.
It is not something to which man comes, but the response
of man to God's invitation. It always embraces the call
of Christ and the imperfect effort of man to comply."[6]
To believe in the church means to express confidence in
the effective summons of Christ, while allowing for the
imperfect performance of those responding.

"Ideally, the universal, or invisible, church and the
local, or visible, church should coincide. There should be
no non-Christian within the local church. In practice,
however, the ideal is never realized."[7] Jesus reminded us
that such would be the case with reference to tares sown
among the wheat, to be sorted out in the final judgment.

The Creed singles out two modifiers for the church,
holy and *catholic* (universal). The holiness of the church
manifests itself most clearly in regard to worship. A company who once called upon the spirit of the sacred tree
now pays homage to the living God.

When we stop to analyze worship, we discover that it
consists of three elements: discovery, celebration, and
commitment. It searches about to find out what God has
been doing, in the redemptive drama of Scripture and
subsequently in the events of history and the lives of those
involved; it rejoices over God's presence in our midst, as
evidenced by his vigorous activity; and it says, "Here am
I, send me," in response to the as yet unfinished task.

The holy community deliberately sets about to discover
God at work in the world, with the intention of express-
ing its appreciation and contributing insofar as possible.
This leads us to the related idea of service (genuine worship fleshes out in willing ministry).

Yet the greatest service the church can render is to be

true to its corporate experience with Christ. It consists of allowing the world to witness how faith matures in the crucible of life. It presses ahead without pretense or sham, asking God's forgiveness and trusting his promises. The church should act as an object lesson for the benefit of others.

The Creed also characterizes the church as *catholic*. Jesus revealed, "I have other sheep, which are not of this fold; I must bring them also, and they shall hear My voice" (John 10:16). He realized how parochial they were in their thinking and meant to impress them with the universal scope of the church.

Jesus applied this conviction concerning the universal nature of the church to those ostracized in his society and the disciples continued the principle by evangelizing a great diversity of people. Thus, Samuel Stone could with good cause reflect:

> Elect from every nation,
>   Yet one o'er all the earth,
> Her charter of salvation
>   One Lord, one faith, one birth;
> One holy name she blesses,
>   Partakes one holy food,
> And to one hope she presses,
>   With every grace endued.

One Lord, Jesus Christ; one faith, in his sustaining grace; one birth, by the Holy Spirit and into life and service together.

"The communion of saints" is probably more of a clarification of the previous phrase than an extension. Not all Christians accepted, even reluctantly, the role of martyr. Defectors multiplied with severe persecution, whittling away at the local congregations.

Some took a less-forgiving attitude than was reflected in the Creed. When they saw these wavering penitents making their way back into the pews, it was too much for them. They protested and when protest failed they separated from the congregation, taking common cause among themselves. It was generally a minority response, losing ground as the memory of persecution eased.

For the most part a more sympathetic feeling prevailed, not to condone the behavior but to recognize the integrity of life together (the communion of saints), and the propriety of reinstating those scattered by foul weather. The Creed reminds us that Christians belong together, even after torn apart by one strain or another.

FORGIVENESS OF SINS

"In a word, the great proclamation of Christianity was and is that God stands always ready to forgive the sins of those who turn to Him in repentance and faith and that they may receive the gift of the Holy Spirit, which means participation in a new quality of life, or to adopt St. Paul's expressive phrase, 'to walk in newness of life.' "[8] The forgiveness of sins and the gift of the Holy Spirit coincide; God forgives us nothing apart from the gift of his life.

"If we confess our sins," the pledge reads, "He is faithful and righteous to forgive us our sins and to cleanse us from all unrighteousness" (I John 1:9). The dual allusion to "our sins" and use of the parallel expression "all unrighteousness" underscore the certainty of the fact. There is no doubt that God offers forgiveness.

Our sins resemble the nails driven through Jesus' hands and feet. They are cruel instruments pounded home with unfeeling efficiency. They strike at Jesus and catch others in their backlash. They remind us of Mary sobbing at her son's feet, the disciples scattered to the wind, and the importune having lost their champion. Sins appear like a contagious disease that soon reaches epidemic proportions.

The sinner fares no better than those he injures. Sooner or later, sin comes home to roost. What we thought to have left forever shows up again on our doorstep.

"All have sinned," Paul concluded, "and fall short of the glory of God" (Rom. 3:23). John adds, "If we say that we have no sin, we are deceiving ourselves, and the truth is not in us" (I John 1:8). They offer no exception to the rule, none at all. At whatever other points we may differ, we all share in the communion of sins.

We may find it convenient to distinguish between sins of commission and sins of omission, the evil we do and the good we leave undone. However, the important thing is not to allow sin to lose its character by shifting from one category to another. The sin of omission is no less sin for failing to qualify as a sin of commission. In fact, I imagine that our worst offenses, were it to be known, would fall into the realm of omission.

Now the Creed chooses to confess itself on the subject of *sins* rather than *sin*, although the one implicates the other. Paul documents our sin by tracing it from our refusal to honor God as God, through degrading practices, to taking pleasure in seeing others carry on such disgraceful behavior (Rom. 1:21–32).

The willingness to confess our sins breaks the way for the forgiveness to follow. "Forgiveness is the will to friendship or love in the face of wrong or injury to one's self," Gardiner Day clarifies, "and the effect of forgiving love in practice is the restoration of friendship or intimacy between the forgiven and the forgiver, between the offender and the offended."[9] It is God's prerogative to forgive, as the offended party, and he chooses to do so. He does not mean to hold our sin against us, if we confess our fault and turn to him in sincere contrition.

Forgiveness was never intended to encourage license, but to provide a wholesome, accepting atmosphere where discipleship can mature. It solicits appreciation for the fact that God has received us in Christ and ministers to us through the Holy Spirit.

GENERAL RESURRECTION

Two death scenes, far more than any others, have captured the imagination of Western man: the death of Socrates and of Jesus. In the thinking of many persons, they strongly resemble each other, virtually to the point that they could be interchanged. These were courageous men, as the thinking goes, true to their convictions in the face of death.

But one could hardly discover two more dissimilar approaches to life and death. "I have put the death of Socrates and the death of Jesus side by side," Oscar Cullmann explains, "for nothing shows better the radical difference between the Greek doctrine of the immortality of the soul and the Christian doctrine of the Resurrection. . . . He [Jesus] cannot obtain this victory by simply living on as an immortal soul, thus fundamentally *not* dying. He can conquer death only by actually dying, by betaking Himself to the sphere of death, the destroyer of life, to the sphere of 'nothingness,' of abandonment by God."[10] Socrates thought of the body as a prison for his immortal soul, a hindrance to realizing what awaited him. Jesus considered the body a gift of God and a facet of personality, a help toward the fulfillment he visualized.

Man, according to Socrates, is a soul and has a body. Jesus held to a much more wholistic idea of man, the body being no less a feature of man than soul or spirit.

Death was therefore regarded differently by the two. Death provided Socrates with release, a long overdue friend. No wonder he faced its arrival with such serenity and quaffed the cup of hemlock. But Jesus struggled with death as a foe, what Paul called "our last enemy" (I Cor. 15:26). It was an adversary to be resisted and eventually vanquished, as Jesus wrestled with the thought of death in Gethsemane and the reality of death on Calvary.

The Christian hope lies not with the immortality of the soul, at least as conceived by Socrates, but with the resurrection of the body. The whole man is the subject of Christ's redemption.

The resurrection "is not like that of certain persons who have risen from the dead but afterwards died," Augustine ties the remaining phrase into the Creed, "but is like the resurrection of Christ's flesh, that is, to Life everlasting."[11] It does not resemble the case of Lazarus but of Christ; it was not an extension of life but a complete triumph over death.

The resurrection also picks up a theme prominent in John's Gospel. "Truly, truly, I say to you," John reports Jesus as saying, "he who believes has eternal life" (John 6:47). Everlasting life is not simply a future but a present reality for the Christian. He now drinks from the water of life, eats of the bread of life, walks in the way of life.

John likewise emphasizes that the Christian hope is not simply for survival but is a continued relationship. "Father, I desire that they also, whom Thou hast given Me, be with Me where I am, in order that they may behold My glory, which Thou hast given Me" (John 17:24). We separate for the time being but unite for eternity—more than a fair exchange for the grieving disciples.

We might argue that everlasting life is more of a qualitative than a quantitative idea, not necessarily the one to the exclusion of the other. The quality of life is enriched by fellowship with the living God and with those sharing in such blessedness.

How does belief in eternal life influence our life presently? The early Christians were noted for their caring for one another, opposing the brutal gladiatorial events, and aiding the importune around them. One person described this life-style as "living their immortality." The life everlasting dips back into the life here and now, to set the pattern, to fix the course, to witness to the future.

The Creed draws to a conclusion, reminding us that the Holy Spirit cannot be satisfied with less than life abundant and everlasting.

RÉSUMÉ

The evangelical raison d'être is the defense of Christian orthodoxy against what Karl Barth described as an anxious openness to the world. Barth observed that this compromising mentality "was forced to make reductions and oversimplifications, to indulge in forgetfulness and carelessness, when it dealt with the exciting and all-important matters of Christian understanding."[12] It was in such a rush to appease the contemporary mood that it impoverished and trivialized the Christian faith.

Orthodox Christianity has witnessed to God's working with man as Father, as Jesus Christ, and as Paraclete. As a prime document of Christian orthodoxy, the Apostles' Creed assumes this three-part outline. While we may uncover differences between the theological emphases of the twentieth-century evangelical movement and the fifth-century editors of the Creed, there is an astonishing amount of overlap in their theological convictions.

In any case, the evangelical stands firm in commitment to historic Christian orthodoxy. The evangelical does not intend to disregard current developments, but to approach them from a Christian perspective and thus to serve better the present age.

READER'S SUMMARY

We review now the evangelical quest for Christian orthodoxy, with particular concern for the aspects of the Creed which we covered in this chapter:

1. The Creed concludes with a confession concerning the Holy Spirit, as extended through areas of his ministry. The orthodox Christian has experienced God at work as a concerned parent, in the life and redeeming ministry of Jesus, and in the fellowship of God's people. The evangelical means to recall us to such a reality.

2. Jesus distinguished between what the world might know of the Spirit's activity (as the origin and sustainer of man's tenuous existence) and that of the disciples (who benefited from the prophetic legacy as an inspired commentary on life), and again as they should experience him at the heart of the Messianic fellowship. Thus, faith in the Holy Spirit implies the confidence that the Almighty is in the process of realizing in the church those concerns for which Jesus interceded on its behalf.

3. The Creed singles out the sanctity and the universality of the Christian community, how it may be kept pure in the present evil age and yet extend its fellowship into every corner of the world. It is a creative tension as the evangelical views the matter, which requires that we

come apart and go with the Lord's presence.

4. We also see the Holy Spirit at work in the forgiveness of sins. The Holy Spirit holds out the prospect of an "accepting atmosphere where discipleship can mature." He encourages us to leave aside our sins for communion with God and service to one another.

5. We likewise view the Spirit in connection with the resurrection of the body and the life everlasting. We understand this to involve the complete recovery of man. The evangelical therefore assumes a much more extravagant hope than simply the idea that life survives death.

6. Anything else that we learn about the modern evangelical movement is incidental to the fact that it exists as an advocate of orthodox Christianity. It understands God in terms of the orthodox creeds, not as an alternative to Scripture and only as the creeds adequately reflect Biblical teaching. It takes special exception to those liberties with the Christian faith which are granted to appease the contemporary mentality.

Part

II

EVANGELICAL ACTION

5

The Centrality of Scripture

"If one began by doubting any statement of the Bible," the fundamentalist believed, "he had started down the slippery slope that would lead to the denial of God and the divinity of Jesus, the loss of certainty of salvation and finally the loss of ethics."[1] Hordern's appraisal may be extreme when applied to the evangelical, but it suggests the direction his thinking is likely to take.

The evangelical predictably assumes a high regard for Biblical authority. He does so out of concern for the consequences that Hordern mentions, but even more for the positive considerations we shall uncover.

RATIONALE

The evangelical reasons that "the Bible is either the word of God or merely a man-made book."[2] We must choose between the two options and follow through on the implications of that choice. If the Bible is the word of God, then we should suppose that it would reflect God's unfailing insight.

Of course, our view of Scripture need not rest on deductive logic alone. We may review Jesus' approach to Holy Writ. "Jesus Christ, so far from rejecting this principle of biblical authority, accepted and built upon it, en-

dorsing it with the greatest emphasis and the full weight
of His authority."[3] The authority of Jesus and that of
Scripture are not in competition but in thorough harmony. "To accept Christ as Lord," Kenneth Kantzer
firms up the position, "and to submit to His teaching
regarding the complete authority of Scripture is consistent."[4]

We see Jesus' estimation of the Scriptures reflected in
the commitment of his disciples. The apostles followed
our Lord in recognizing the abiding authority of the Old
Testament over the people of God. The church proclaimed the Jewish Scriptures as a Christian book, but by
treating those Scriptures as God-given law for the guid-
ance of its life.[5]

The church also accepted the New Testament as an
extension of Scripture. Thus Peter refers to "our beloved
brother Paul," whose letters were thought to contain
"some things hard to understand, which the untaught
and unstable distort, as they do also the rest of the Scriptures" (II Peter 3:15). And the church fathers acknowl-
edged the New Testament as authoritative teaching.

The evangelical's strategy is a calculated one. He
weighs the implications of Scripture as the Word of God,
listens to Jesus' teaching concerning Scripture, and observes the response of the church to Holy Writ. All these
considerations seem to urge him to take Biblical authority
seriously.

HISTORICAL PERSPECTIVE

Christian orthodoxy took more liberty with the idea of
Biblical authority than many of its more recent evangelical champions have been inclined to do.

There is in all orthodoxy the faith that God has revealed himself, particularly in the events recorded in the Bible. This special revelation begins with the choosing of the Jews and culminates in the man Jesus. But there has been no final agreement on how God is revealed in the Bible or in what form it is an inspired book. In fact these are questions which did not become burning issues until the twentieth century.[6]

The questions became "burning issues" with the rise of the fundamentalist/modernist controversy.

Luther is often cited for the qualifications he placed on Biblical authority. He insisted on the preference of Scripture and personal conviction over pope and council, while questioning the authenticity of Esther and Revelation, the value of James, and the accuracy of details. He went so far as to propose that another New Testament might be written if one could assemble a group of equally dedicated writers.

Luther's position was not, strictly speaking, normative for contemporary evangelical thought. What it illustrates is that the line of conviction could at that time be drawn with less care. "But if the Bible is the authority by which you vanquish king and pope," Hordern acknowledges the inevitable, "you cannot treat the Bible as freely as did Luther. To protect their authority the Protestants claimed that the Bible was the only infallible authority, and unlike that of pope and king, the literal word of God."[7]

The impact of Protestant orthodoxy has been interpreted differently. Some saw it as working together with the destructive rationalism of the time; others viewed it as a creative Christian development. Probably there is some truth to both estimates.[8]

In any case, Protestant fundamentalism took its key not only from Scripture itself but from the polemic intent

given to it by the seventeenth century. Roman Catholic
fundamentalism chose the other side of the watershed
with its emphasis on the authority of the church. Both
alike resisted the threat to Christian orthodoxy as understood within their respective communions.

The contemporary evangelical concern has surfaced in
various connections: the fundamentalist movement,[9] pie-
tistic tradition, Reformed fellowship, charismatic awakening, impetus of Vatican II, and indigenous church
movements, to mention just a few. It reflects the abiding
conviction that we take Biblical authority seriously and
views that need with reference to the fundamental-
ist/modernist struggle. What previously passed as questions have taken on the nature of burning issues.

THE AUTHORITY ISSUE

We can simplify the question of authority in Christian
thought by identifying three sources: Scripture, church,
and reason. These have also been the respective options
of orthodox Protestantism, traditional Roman Catholicism, and liberalism (whether Protestant or Roman Catholic). These three categories are helpful, providing we do
not assume that the sources are mutually exclusive.

"The Bible, I say, the Bible only, is the religion of
Protestants."[10] One could hardly come more quickly to
the seat of the authority issue. While God may be said
to reveal himself variously, the Scriptures alone deserve to
be honored as God's word. Neither church tradition nor
conventional understanding can make that claim. "For
the written word is but the completion or reflection of the
Living Word," Alan Stibbs concludes. "It is, so to speak,
the halo round His head in which His glory finds visible
or intelligible, because verbal, expression."[11] Thus he
grants Scripture its privileged position.

The traditional Roman Catholic prefers a different question than implied in the Protestant's answer. Does the Scripture give us the church, he wants to know, or does the church provide us with the Scripture? It seems evident enough to him that the latter is in fact the case. The church, for the Roman Catholic, is virtually the extension of the incarnation, the body of which Christ serves as head and the pope acts as his vicar.

The liberal, of whatever communion, qualifies the Christian teaching to accommodate the current understanding of the time. He does not mean to deny Holy Writ or Holy Church a role, but demands that they generously share their prerogatives with others. He claims to accept truth wherever it may be discovered but is left with the problem of arbitrating among conflicting points of view.

The fact is that we never really appeal to one of these sources to the total exclusion of the others. It is more a matter of emphasis, a preference to err (if needs be) in one direction rather than in another. For instance, the Protestant does not believe that the sun actually rises and sets, taking the Biblical expression as descriptive of how things appear to us. He allows reason to inform his understanding of Scripture.

Similarly, when the Reformation adopted the *sola Scriptura* theme, it was designed to correct the undue emphasis that had been placed on tradition. The Reformers felt that beliefs were being promulgated contrary to the best understanding of Scripture, while Biblical truths were ignored or distorted. *Sola Scriptura* never meant that the church fathers should be repudiated. On the contrary, the Reformation "had great respect for what was ancient in the church, especially in the Anglican and the Lutheran churches."[12]

The fundamentalists of repute likewise tempered their

appeal to Scripture in connection with the best insights of their time. "We hope that the evidence adduced will be sufficient to show that the general reliability of the Old Testament documents has not been impaired by recent discovery outside the Old Testament," Robert Dick Wilson details his intent. "The civil, criminal and constitutional laws agree with what the civilization of the ancient nations surrounding Palestine would suppose; while the ceremonial, moral, and religious laws are differentiated from those of others by their genesis in a monotheistic belief and a divine revelation."[13] He observed a rigorous academic discipline in his study and drew upon only what could be advanced in that fashion.

The point is that regardless of how we emphasize one source over another, we blend them together in some mix, and here we refine the idea of authority. Some Protestants are quite "catholic" in the weight they grant to a given tradition, and some Roman Catholics are rather "protestant" in the normative role they give to Scripture. One could align certain Protestants and Roman Catholics as over against certain others of the two communions on the authority concern. Moreover, it appears that the evangelical resurgence inevitably tips the scales toward a solid appreciation of the normative role of Biblical revelation. The evangelical stragegy is predictable in this regard.

BASIC PROPOSITIONS

We can now take a more deliberate look at the evangelical position on Scripture. Not every evangelical will state his perspective in precisely the same way, but there is seldom much deviation from the basic propositions set forth by Kenneth Kantzer, current dean of Trinity Evangelical Divinity School:[14]

1. The ultimate object of all Biblical revelation is God as a person. It "is not so much to make man wise as it is to bring him into a direct encounter with God as a person, and to evoke from him a response of love and obedience to God." This is not what one might expect from the charge of Bibliolatry so carelessly thrown the evangelical way. The alternative subjects, as the evangelical sees them, are not the Bible or God, but the God of Scripture or a divinity of our own making.

2. Biblical revelation is by divine acts. It "is the unfolding of the gracious acts of God in behalf of sinful man." It qualifies as redemptive history.

3. Biblical revelation culminates in Jesus Christ. "As revealer, Christ's uniqueness lies in the completeness and finality of His revelation. Others beside Him spoke the Word of God; but He was, in truth, *God speaking.*" The evangelical repudiates any dichotomy suggested between the truth of Jesus and that of Scripture.

4. Biblical revelation also includes God's interpretation of the events. God "is a living, acting, speaking person who enters into social intercourse and fellowship with man and who gives to men a revelation, His own divine interpretation of the meaning of things." God reveals himself in word as well as deed.

5. This revelation is brought to men by the Bible. "The Bible thus becomes the means through which revelations given directly to prophets in Old Testament history and to apostles in New Testament history are made available for the needy sinner of every succeeding generation." Such truth may not be thought to reside in general revelation or even without impairment in the tradition of the church but in the normative canon of Scripture.

6. Revelation must be subjectively appropriated. "The objective side of the divine work of revelation needs to be supplemented by the internal subjective work of the

Spirit of God." We do encounter God through the Scripture, but this fact does not rule out the Bible *as* an objective revelation.

7. The authority of the Bible is known by revelation. It is privileged information made eminently clear through the Biblical writers. "There is no other question on which the apostolic writers are in such clear agreement or on which they speak with more freedom or assurance than upon the doctrine of the authority of the Scriptures."

8. The authority of the Bible is derived from its divine inspiration. "All Scripture is inspired by God and profitable for teaching, for reproof, for correction, for training in righteousness; that the man of God may be adequate, equipped for every good work" (II Tim. 3:16–17), and "no prophecy of Scripture is a matter of one's own interpretation, for no prophecy was ever made by an act of human will, but men moved by the Holy Spirit spoke from God" (II Peter 1:20–21). "The Apostle does not teach that the Bible was dictated by God," Kantzer corrects a misunderstanding of the evangelical position, "but rather that it was produced by the prophets through a divine energizing and enabling." It is the Word of God in the words of men.

9. The Bible must be rightly interpreted. "A Biblical view of inspiration does not rule out either historical or textual criticism," Kantzer argues. "Rather it demands legitimate application of these studies to a proper understanding of the Bible." Commonly designated as a historical-grammatical approach to Scripture, it seeks to discover the meaning of what was revealed in Biblical culture for our own time.

10. The fact of Biblical authority is the foundation for a valid theology. "Genuine evangelical theology is based upon the teaching of the whole Bible received as the

authoritative written Word of God. Its theology rests solidly upon the holy Scriptures, for they and they alone are not only able to make us wise unto salvation but are also possessed of God-given authority and are profitable for doctrine." The evangelical strategy could not be more clearly accented.

AUTOGRAPHS, VERBAL INSPIRATION, AND INERRANCY

We might leave the evangelical thrust at this point but for three recurring expressions in the pertinent literature. They are the references to autographs, verbal inspiration, and inerrancy. It is common, although certainly not universal, for evangelicals to consider the original writings to be without error even in such matters as historical detail. This attitude reflects an awareness of certain difficulties in the present text, the general absence of substantial problems, and the probability that the transmission of the manuscripts could account for the relatively minor concerns. Whether he introduces the idea of autographs or not, the evangelical fails to see why we should revel in skepticism when the bulk of evidence points toward the credibility of Scripture.

The evangelical is even more predictable in his appeal to verbal inspiration. Scripture details not only the acts of God but their meaning. He does not necessarily hold a dictation theory, where the personality of the prophet would be suppressed, or any theory in particular. He only wants to affirm in the clearest of terms that God spoke as well as acted, and that the significance of his actions would be unintelligible under any other circumstance.

The idea of inerrancy kicks up considerable controversy. Some evangelicals prefer the term "infallible" for that reason, while others feel this substitution would grant an unwarranted concession. Both agree that the Bible is without error in connection with what it means to cover and in the fashion it intends to do so.

What does such a confidence imply for Biblical accuracy in historical matters? The evangelical feels that he has a high stake in history. He urges us to consider the literary, cultural, and theological factors involved but as part of a comprehensive historical investigation. Either God acted in history, the evangelical reasons, or we know nothing of his activity.

This does not imply that the Scripture could pass as a textbook on science. What it says is stated from the viewpoint of an interested observer. The Bible speaks in "the language of the market place, of social gatherings, and of the chance conversation. It is that basic vocabulary and style which the masses use to carry on their daily communication," in contrast to "that jargon developed in the history of science . . . which enables men of each science to communicate more accurately, conveniently, and economically."[15] Thus, if we can determine that a certain Biblical number was used to signify "a large body of people," we would not hold out for the literal figure in the fashion of those whom Bernard Ramm calls "hyperorthodox." The evangelical means to sustain Christian orthodoxy, not press it to some absurdity.

READER'S SUMMARY

We now attempt to summarize several of the basic conclusions reached in regard to the evangelical strategy:

1. The evangelical takes as his point of leverage a high view of Biblical authority and holds tenaciously to that conviction. It seems to him that either God has taken the initiative to reveal himself or our faith is vain.

2. We should not think of this as an arbitrary stratagem. It seems to follow from understanding the Scripture as God's Word, the attitude assumed by Jesus, and the response of the church to Scripture.

3. The contemporary evangelical acknowledges that he has pressed for a sharper definition of Biblical authority than was uniformly represented in former orthodox speculation. He does not want to strain the issue unnecessarily but realizes that Christian orthodoxy must continue to respond to the challenges thrown at it.

4. Scripture assumes primacy in evangelical thinking, as the normative guide for faith and practice. We allow the historical revelation if God is to take preference over tradition and reason in molding our understanding of the world and constructing a life-style.

5. Evangelicals share a core of beliefs related to their understanding of Scripture. They view God as the ultimate object of revelation; Scripture as recording the acts of God and his explanation of their significance; Christ as the focus of Scripture; revelation as objectively inspired and subjectively appreciated. These beliefs form the basis of a valid evangelical theology.

6. Finally, the evangelical expresses concern over the Biblical autographs, verbal inspiration, and inerrancy. He holds that the Bible speaks accurately on the subjects it means to address and in the manner it chooses to do so. It is the Word of God in the words of men.

6

Evangelism

William Hordern understands "the heart of fundamentalism" to be "its concern for salvation."[1] The evangelical wholeheartedly shares the commitment to evangelism. "To be evangelical means to believe that we are justified only by grace through faith in Him who suffered and died for our sins," Donald Bloesch explains, adding that *evangelical* "also refers to the spirit in which this message is proclaimed, the spirit of zeal and earnestness."[2] Evangelism has become the anticipated concern of the evangelical.

Carl F. H. Henry ties the evangelical commitment to evangelism to the lapse of interest elsewhere. "During these lean years of liberalism," he reflects back on the situation, "the call of evangelism went begging in the regular churches, and therefore passed by default to independent and interdenominational enterprises."[3] When forsaken by the church at large, the evangelical made a marked contribution in keeping evangelism alive.

THE FOCUS

Some persons confuse the command to evangelize with the cultural mandate. God instructed man to subdue the world and rule over it (Gen. 1:28), from which we derive the idea of a cultural mandate. It implies that we weave a human fabric into creation so as to benefit and enrich life.

God has not relaxed the conditions of the cultural mandate, but sin intervened. "There is no distinction," Paul concludes; "for all have sinned and fall short of the glory of God" (Rom. 3:22–23). The evangelical realizes that we cannot press ahead as if nothing had happened, as though there were no sin or continuing alienation from God as a result.

Sin permeates the entire nature of man, which is the best understanding of the idea of *total depravity*. It "does not mean that sinners are as bad as they can possibly be —the man who beats his wife does not beat her all the time, and the person who cheats on his income tax does not cheat in every imaginable fashion, or steal at every opportunity. Nor does it mean that men cannot and do not perform any acts of general goodness—even the murderer may be a kind, thoughtful, and generous husband and father."[4] But total depravity does imply that life can never be free at any point from the influence of sin.

This healthy respect for sin has long been a trademark of the evangelical perspective. When others tried to explain man's dilemma on simply psychological or sociological grounds, the evangelical took issue. He persisted with the idea that the problem is basically a religious one.

The evangelical couples with his emphasis on sin the fact that man is lost apart from Christ. "Unless the non-evangelical understands this absolute seriousness of the manner in which the evangelical understands what is at stake in theology, the nonevangelical will persistently misunderstand or ridicule or belittle the evangelical," Ramm warns, "but until the evangelical can be shown that the difference of saved and lost is not absolute, that the difference between the Church and the world is not one of a kind, and that Christian and non-Christian represent but degrees of awareness of a heritage, he will still think in terms of saved and lost which in turn will govern the entire way he looks at the theological enterprise."[5] A person is either saved or lost, and if lost, then in need of Christ.

We used to hear a lot about the lost*ness* of man, which seemed to imply that man was grappling through the maze of life. Or someone would comment on the human sickness, as if we might expect a recovery at any moment. These ideas appear to the evangelical as part truths at best, terrible perversions otherwise. He views man as a willful renegade from God, lost but not forsaken.

We might also sharpen the distinction between loving our neighbor and making disciples. "The Great Commission neither explains, nor exhausts, nor supersedes the Great Commandment. What it does is to add to the command of neighbor-love and neighbor service a new and urgent Christian dimension. If we truly love our neighbor we shall without doubt tell him the Good News of Jesus. But equally if we truly love our neighbor we shall not stop there."[6] The evangelical appreciates the fact that evangelism neither replaces nor embodies the love and service of others, but something is wrong with our love-service ministry when it neglects evangelism.

"If a brother or sister is without clothing and in need of daily food" and we ask God's blessing upon the person as an alternative to meeting the person's need, "what use is that?" (James 2:15–16). The evangelical option is neither faith nor works but a faith that works. He sees the Great Commission as an intricate part but not the whole of his neighbor love and service. He remembers the words of the Lord that "man shall not live on bread alone, but

on every word that proceeds out of the mouth of God"
(Matt. 4:4). One must care for the whole man.

The evangelical thus observes the distinct call of God
to evangelize and senses the urgency of heeding it. He
feels called to dedicate himself to an unending task and
remorseful for having been so lax concerning it. "We
confess with some that we have often denied our call and
failed in our mission, by becoming conformed to the
world or by withdrawing from it," reads an excerpt from
the Lausanne Covenant, "yet we rejoice that even when
borne by earthen vessels the Gospel is still a precious
treasure. To the task of making that treasure known in
the power of the Holy Spirit we desire to dedicate ourselves anew."[7] The evangelical is struck by the awesome
nature of the undertaking and his shortcoming. "Who
are we to take up such a responsibility?" he asks himself,
only to have the first question crowded out by a second:
"Who are we not to abide by the Lord's commission?"

So the evangelical goes not always *triumphantly* but
somehow about the charge to evangelize. Even his critics
begrudgingly grant him that much.

COMPONENTS IN EVANGELISM

John Stott outlines the nature of evangelism as regards
the gospel events, witnesses, promises, and demands.[8]
There are the critical events, primarily the death and
resurrection of Jesus. "The gospel is good news. It is news
because of an event anchored in history and human experience. It is good because 'God was in Christ reconciling
the world to himself.' "[9] Something of the greatest importance took place and evangelism testifies to its continuing significance.

The religious syncretist likes to play the sound-alike,

look-alike game when discussing the gospel events. Jesus' crucifixion seems to him simply another case of martyr-dom, and the resurrection just one more miracle meant to support some religious claim. He fails to appreciate the distinctive nature of the gospel events and therefore the significance of evangelism as well.

Declaring, "This Jesus God raised up again, to which we are all witnesses" (Acts 2:32), Peter takes us from the gospel events to the persons who bore witness to them.

These gospel witnesses reported what they saw as the culmination of God's working with a particular people. The Almighty had called out a peculiar people to himself, sustained them through the most trying experience, and taught them his ways. There has been no comparable instance among the peoples of the world.[10]

The witness also related to the extraordinary life and ministry of Jesus. The resurrection appeared as a fitting climax to the advent of Christ rather than a bizarre turn of events at its conclusion.

The idea of witness further implies the continuing significance of the things that had come to pass. It alerted persons to the relevance of such matters, the possibility of acting upon them, and the tragedy of ignoring one's opportunity.

So when the disciples came to nominate a substitute for Judas, they selected from those who had "accom-panied us all the time that the Lord Jesus went in and out among us" to "become a witness with us of His resurrec-tion" (Acts 1:21–22). They assumed the course of events in Jesus' life as the latest chapter in God's working with the chosen people and as reaching out to embrace people everywhere.

There are also the gospel promises. The death-resurrec-tion was a historical event but not that alone. It can result in a profound transformation of life for those who appropriate its truth. "For if we have become united with Him in the likeness of His death," Paul reasons, "certainly we shall be also in the likeness of His resurrection, knowing this, that our old self was crucified with Him, that our body of sin might be done away with, that we should no longer be slaves to sin" (Rom. 6:5–6). The bonds were broken and lie useless at our feet. All the years of enslavement pass, never to return again.

We likewise enjoy the promise of life with Christ. "Now Christ has been raised from the dead, the first fruits of those who are asleep" (I Cor. 15:20). If Christ is the firstfruits, then we shall be harvested at his coming. As a down payment on the full principle, the resurrection of Jesus provides the pledge of final redemption.

"Even so consider yourselves to be dead to sin," Paul adds, "but alive to God in Christ Jesus" (Rom. 6:11). The promise concerns not only the eventual triumph but its present reality. We now experience the abundant life of persons freed to serve. We are alive to God as a result of the crucifixion-resurrection. Old things have passed away, all things are refreshingly new.

Turning from the gospel promises, we finally consider the gospel demands. The first of these is repentance. When Peter's audience was pierced through by his words and asked what they might do by way of response, the apostle demanded that they repent (Acts 2:38). "Repentance is a realization of one's sinful state and condition, a feeling of godly sorrow or genuine remorse for sin, and a determination to abandon sin. It is not merely feeling sorrow for sin because of certain undesirable consequences that have occurred. It is regretting one's acts and thoughts because they are an offense against a holy God."[11] It is also the determination to forge on in communion with God from that point on.

The second command concerns faith. "Believe in the Lord Jesus," Paul admonished the Philippian jailer, "and you shall be saved, you and your household" (Acts 16:31). Christian faith is trust in Christ for salvation. Jesus is the object; salvation, the result. The evangelical has stressed the vicarious nature of Christ's ministry. "He made Him who knew no sin to be sin on our behalf," the writer confides, "that we might become the righteousness of God in Him" (II Cor. 5:21). His death effectively introduced our deliverance.

The moral example theory fails the test of Scripture. We do not simply model our lives after Jesus but accept what he has already accomplished on our behalf. We trust in his grace rather than in our works.

Now, salvation is not primarily a psychological or sociological reality but a religious one. It is true that *salvation* implies a certain health of being, whether in regard to oneself or in relationship to others, but the primary reference is religious.

Therefore, we accept Jesus' ministry as effective in mediating between God and man. It provides us with a certain access to God's presence. "Let us therefore draw near with confidence to the throne of grace" by faith, "that we may receive mercy and may find grace to help in time of need" (Heb. 4:16). Salvation points us first toward God, then to meeting our personal and social needs.

The kerygma likewise stresses baptism as at least a public token of repentance and faith in Christ. The central issue is nonetheless Jesus. We do not repent for repentance' sake; we do not have faith in faith; we do not baptize for some merit in the act itself. The gospel demands that we face up to Christ. What will we do with Jesus?

The discussion has taken us from the gospel events, through witnesses and promises, to commands. The evangelical, whatever else he may have lacked, has kept the course of evangelism before him. He stresses the saving work of Christ, as a faithful witness, enthusiastic over the promises of the gospel and feeling the weight of its obligations. He appreciates the counsel, "Preach as a dying man to dying men." No one has to convince the evangelical of the urgency of confronting man with the claims of Christ.

The Kerygma

We have referred to the kerygma from time to time as the proclamation of the early church. While our previous emphasis was on content, we now consider the process involved with heralding the gospel. We declare what God has done, means to do, or will bring to pass. "To 'evangelize' in biblical usage does not mean to win converts (as it usually does when we use the word) but simply to announce the good news, irrespective of the results."[12] The emphasis is on the gracious offer of God instead of on our response or lack of response to it.

I am reminded of a story concerning the best-known of contemporary evangelicals and evangelists, Billy Graham. It seems that some were needling him about the questionable staying power of his converts, to which he responded that one should not expect much of Graham converts, since only those converted by God would manage. Graham's response is characteristic of evangelical thinking. He considers it his obligation to publish the glad tidings; God will have to provide any increase.

This kerygmatic approach to evangelism relegates methods to a secondary place. Shall we further mass evangelism or foster personal evangelism? Shall we begin with the large urban area or carry the message to the un-touched villages? These questions are important but should not obscure the heart of the issue, which is to proclaim the gospel in any way it seems appropriate.

The evangelical cannot speak on behalf of other religious groups. It may be that some of them have no evangelistic concern and properly so. But it must then be added that this is a point at which orthodox Christianity differs. The Christian faith, as evangelically understood, *is* an evangelistic faith.

It does in fact seem strange to the evangelical that so many urge tolerance as a religious ideal, while being intolerant in other critical areas. Who would allow an ailing member of the family to be treated by anyone who cares to do so in any way the person sees fit? Why then such lack of discrimination when it comes to matters of eternity? It could perhaps be excused if we lacked the sure word of the gospel, but the evangelical does not waver on that count.

Does this uncompromising attitude rule out dialogue? No. Time and again The Acts reveals that Paul chose to reason with his hearers (Acts 17:2, 17; 18:4, 19; 19:8–9; 20:7; 24:25). He persuaded as well as proclaimed, as part of an interaction with the views of others.

The evangelical is similarly inclined. "The defenders of conservativism gladly take their case into the arena of logic and reason because they believe that it is precisely here that they have their best case."[13] Here in the course of human events (where God has taken the trouble to disclose his truth, where man must own up to his responsibilities, and where perspectives clash) is the arena where truth must triumph over error.

The evangelical does not think that he knows everything there is to be known or that what he knows is comprehended in full. He allows that an interchange must be two-sided and that each participant can learn from the other. He also appreciates, at least in his better moments, how culturally bound is his own understanding of Biblical truth. He supposes that his faith can be greatly enriched as he tries to share his insights with others.

The evangelical is also sensitive that the gospel came to him by virtue of some inexplicable turn in God's providence, such as when Paul had discovered first one door closed, and then another, before entertaining the summons to Macedonia (Acts 16:6–10). Then the good news moved west into Europe, with the result that some heard it before others. It was a twist of providence, nothing more, and certainly no detriment to dialogue or cause to feel condescending.

Nonetheless, the evangelical sides with Hendrik Kraemer in the opinion that "we are bold enough to call men out from them [other religions] to the feet of Christ. We do so because we believe that in him alone is the full salvation which man needs."[14] The evangelical feels that he serves no one by watering down the desperate condition of man or God's gracious provision. He thus takes evangelism in stride. It seems to him the natural complement to Christian faith.

READER'S SUMMARY

We have reached our immediate destination and can sum up:

1. The evangelical's concern for salvation flows from his loyalty to the gospel: If Christ died for our sins, then we must share the good news with others. However, it also reflects the lapse of interest in other circles and the evangelical's burden to reintroduce evangelism to its

rightful place of importance.

2. It follows that we cannot pursue the cultural mandate to subdue the earth without regard for the fact that sin has intervened. "This healthy respect for sin has long been a trademark of the evangelical perspective."

3. The evangelical acutely senses the fact that man is lost apart from Christ. While shrinking from the overwhelming demands of the Great Commission, he feels compelled to heed its call. He is constrained by the lost condition of man and urged on by the compassion of Christ.

4. The evangelical asks us to consider the gospel events, witnesses, promises, and demands. He stresses what God has brought to pass, our responsibility to make it known, and the opportunity and obligation that falls on those who hear. He reasons that God's initiative demands an appropriate response all the way along the line.

5. The accent rests on our obligation to proclaim the gospel. We ought to be more concerned with making the gospel known than tabulating the results. God can be trusted to make the most of any faithful endeavor, so as to stop men in their flight.

7

Missions

The evangelical's interest in missions grows logically out of his stress on evangelism. Missions is evangelism viewed universally.

I seldom reflect on missions for very long without my thoughts going back to the five young men who perished at the hands of Auca Indians in January of 1956. The word raced through evangelical circles like a brush fire, alerting them to the tragedy and triumph. Soon literally hundreds of persons would pledge themselves to take the places of these few who gave their lives on a remote sandy beach. The blood of the martyr had again become the seed of the church.

Some of my nonevangelical acquaintances reacted quite differently. They immediately assumed that proper precautions had been ignored on the way to a hasty and ill-advised contact. I wondered at the time how these folk could be so assured as to what had happened but realized that they were working with an evangelical stereotype.

In any case, the motivation involved in this instance is easier to document than the adequacy of procedures. Jim Elliot wrote one summer, while enrolled as a student at Wheaton College:

"He makes His ministers a flame of fire." Am I ignitable? God deliver me from the dread asbestos of "other things." Saturate me with the oil of the Spirit that I may be a flame. But flame is transient, often short-lived. Canst thou bear this, my soul—short life? In me there dwells the Spirit of the Great Short-Lived, whose zeal for God's house consumed Him. "Make me Thy fuel, Flame of God."[1]

The evangelical accepts a brief journey if in good company and on a worthy destination. He would prefer to walk the few steps with Christ in pursuit of Christ's calling than the long, winding road of rebellion. He would surrender his threescore and ten years for a strategic ministry. Such an attitude breeds a missionary fervor.

Pattern for Missions

Ralph Winter outlines what he describes as "cross-cultural evangelism," which is, as I see it, a synonym for missions.[2] The first variety of evangelism, according to Winter, shares with those of one's own culture (E–1); the second bridges to a similar culture (E–2); the final instance reaches to a radically strange culture (E–3). These cultural differences are not necessarily established by geographical distance. Those culturally similar may be relatively remote, or two very dissimilar groups may live side by side.

Winter also distinguishes between cultural distance and walls of prejudice. "It is clear that Jesus is referring primarily neither to geography nor walls of prejudice when he lists *Judea, Samaria,* and *the ends of the earth,*" Winter explains. "Had he been talking prejudice, Samaria would have come last. He would have said, 'in Judea, in all the world, and *even in Samaria.*' "[3] The Samaritans were similar in culture but separated by a chasm of prejudice.

The evangelical has seldom been satisfied for long with

E–1 evangelism. His fervor spread the gospel over Europe, awaited a vision of the continents beyond, and plunged into the modern missionary movement. While less evangelically-minded folk competed for the pulpits, staffed the seminaries, and coveted the administrative positions at home, the evangelical carried the brunt of the task of bearing the word to the ends of the earth.

He had more than a little success, seeing that the rapid Christian growth areas today are not in the traditional Christian centers but elsewhere. For all of the criticism properly leveled at the evangelical effort, the seed was planted and a bountiful harvest followed.

And the evangelical movement shows relatively little intention of cutting back on its missionary activity. As the missionary budget in many denominations levels off or drops backward, the distinctively evangelical groups seem to push on from one high of support to another. The Lausanne Covenant declared:

More than 2,700 million people, which is more than two-thirds of mankind, have yet to be evangelized. We are ashamed that so many have been neglected; it is a standing rebuke to the whole church. . . . We are convinced that this is the time for churches and para-church agencies to pray earnestly for the unreached and to launch new efforts to achieve world evangelization.[4]

One of the major obstacles to seeing the continuing need for E–2 and E–3 evangelism is our failure to recognize the extent of subcultures. "God apparently loves diversity of certain kinds," Winter allows. "But in any case this diversity means evangelists have to work harder."[5] Harder and with greater sensitivity! The various ethnic pieces that go into any regional mosaic taxes the imagination and energy of the concerned evangelist.

Winter wonders if we are prepared to accept the fact that most prospective converts have difficulty fitting into our established churches and that they constitute a case for E–2 evangelism. As an example, he questions the exodus of churches into suburbia, following those of like culture rather than ministering to persons of dissimilar culture.

John Wesley's approach to the English miners is a good instance of E–2 evangelism. He encouraged them to hold their own gatherings, sing their own kind of songs, reach their own sort of people. Or we may recall the more recent phenomenon of the Jesus People, who have founded hundreds of congregations and appealed to thousands of counterculture persons.

The differences in age groups may also require something of an E–2 evangelism. These generation gaps tend to close, given time and a sympathetic understanding, but we cannot always afford to ignore them for the time being. This realization no doubt has motivated the evangelical's emphasis on youth ministry, evangelism, and fellowship.[6]

E–3 evangelism moves us into areas that have been largely impervious to the gospel, such as the Muslim world, behind the Iron Curtain, and the chaotic realm of the cults. It encounters situations that seem strange and sometimes threatening. It may even evolve practices that run counter to the expected pattern, like some African converts who pray five times daily and worship on Friday.

The evangelical has been becoming increasingly sensitive to the conditions necessary for doing effective E–3 evangelism. The lessons have not come easily and are still being acquired, but the evangelical impetus to missions has provided the opportunity and the perseverance that promises even better results in the future.

OCCASION FOR MISSIONS

One may think of missions as a burden, a challenge, or an opportunity. The evangelical views it as something of a challenge *and* an opportunity. According to J. Herbert Kane,

The real tragedy does not lie in the closed countries that we can't enter, but in the open countries we don't enter. Closed countries are God's responsibility. We can safely leave them with Him. Open countries are our responsibility, and we neglect them at our peril. We should be up and doing. Time *is* short. The fields *are* white. The laborers *are* few. It is both foolish and futile to spend our time lamenting the few doors that are closed, while we refuse to enter the many doors that are open.[7]

Kane's comments are quite typical of the evangelical temperament, as he shakes off inertia and picks out a likely target.

The major impetus, as suggested in the quotation, is the sovereign will of God at work. The evangelical takes it that God is still active in the affairs of men and nations, and most significantly when things appear dismal to us. "William Carey was pleading the cause of world missions during the French Revolution, which threatened to engulf the whole of Europe. The first American missionaries sailed for India in 1812, the year that war broke out between Britain and the United States. Hudson Taylor first arrived in China in 1853 as the Taiping Rebellion was getting under way—a rebellion that lasted fifteen years and took at least twenty million lives."[8] As a friend who had been reared of missionary parents was fond of repeating, "The wrath of man shall praise Thee" (Ps.

76:10). He sensed God bringing his sovereign will to bear in the midst of struggle and seeming chaos.

The evangelical couples the idea of human responsibility with that of divine sovereignty. "Closed countries are God's responsibility," as Kane put it. "Open countries are our responsibility." The evangelical finds it puzzling when persons complain over the heathen being damned and do nothing to help the matter. He supposes that God is already at work to rectify the problem and means that we should join in the enterprise.

God loves man in all his seemingly endless variety and encourages the prodigal to come home. He bids us turn from sin and bring our gifts to serve the living God.

We should not hesitate. "Behold, now is 'the acceptable time,'" Paul declared, "behold, now is 'the day of salvation'" (II Cor. 6:2). We can never assume a second chance, let alone a third or fourth. This matter of reconciliation to God takes priority over everything else. "For what does it profit a man to gain the whole world, and forfeit his soul?" Jesus inquired. "For what shall a man give in exchange for his soul?" (Mark 8:36–37).

The evangelical sees missions as a challenging opportunity of joining the Almighty in his work, in the place that is the Almighty's choosing, at his time, with his power at our disposal. The scales are already tipped in favor of the person sincerely committed to the will of God. Even the discouragements seem a prelude to blessing and the harvest of fruit in God's appointed time.

CHRIST AND CULTURE

Missions inevitably involve the Christ and culture issue and the evangelical predictably places his accent on Christ.[9] There are two reasons for his preference, the first being the problem he senses with conventional idolatry. That is, culture enslaves those who make it their prime consideration.

The evangelical is of course not alone in his warning of the tyrannical tendency of culture. "Culture necessarily degenerates where it is made God," observes Emil Brunner. "Culture-idolatry is the sure road to cultural decay. If culture is to become and to remain truly human, it must have a culture-transcending center."[10]

The second reason for the evangelical's preference relates to the liberating nature of the gospel. "If therefore the Son shall make you free," Jesus contrasts the option with its alternative, "you shall be free indeed" (John 8:36). "It is precisely the man whose first concern is not culture but the kingdom of God that has the necessary distance from cultural aims and the necessary perspective to serve them in freedom and to grasp that order which prevents the various sections of civilization from monopolizing the totality of life."[11] The Christian's concern for the world to come acts as a leverage on the present world.

The evangelical sees as the genuine alternatives Christ *and* culture or a lack in both. The universal figure of Christ offers the best prospect of liberating man for his cultural task, while an unbridled culture tends to inhibit life. Those who can transcend culture prove to be its most effective contributors.

This realization brings us to the question of how faith influences culture. In some ways the result is minimal and in others quite complete. The components of culture remain much the same. That is, the various building blocks that distinguish one culture from another may be rearranged somewhat but otherwise left undisturbed. Take the preference for one food staple over another: the Irish potato, Oriental rice, the West African yam. One may offer up grace before partaking of any of these, as an expression of one's faith.

Extend the illustration a little further. I can recall how upset a conscientious housewife would get with persons who turned up unexpectedly at mealtime. "They should know better," she would complain. The West African takes a much different attitude and treats the unplanned-for guest as if the person were invited. The concept of hospitality differs among cultures, but there is no reason to believe that the Christian faith cannot adjust from one set of social amenities to another. The components remain much the same in any case.

Some have estimated that these building blocks consti-tute over 90 percent of what we understand as culture. Over 90 percent! Somehow we get the idea that there must be some radical displacement of culture when Christ moves in, but the preponderance of culture can be adopted by the convert.

There are some things the Christian should reject out of deference to the Word of God. Paul protested the practice of joining in pagan festivity: "I say that the things which the Gentiles sacrifice, they sacrifice to de-mons, and not to God; and I do not want you to become sharers in demons" (I Cor. 10:20). He drew the issue sharply, as we all must on occasion.

There are other cultural considerations that faith sim-ply elevates to a higher point of reference than they previously enjoyed. Accordingly, Paul admonished, "let each individual among you also love his own wife even as himself; and let the wife see to it that she respect her husband" (Eph. 5:33). Marriage takes on the ideal that was set forth by Christ and the church.

On the other hand, culture may rob faith of its original significance. Julian Hartt explains: "The Christ-epic is still with us [as] the expression of some element or aspect of that 'sacred history,' " but less than the former significance.[12] That is to say, culture has watered down the Christian message.

We see that the Christian faith can leave the bulk of culture essentially unaltered, except where it runs into conflict with Biblical imperatives, and so long as we resist the erosion of Christian meaning. Christ blends culture into a mix that reflects a love of God and our neighbor as ourselves—where idolatry and tyranny are banished and man is free indeed.

SUMMARY

We have discovered the evangelical concern for evangelism and its related expansion to missions. The evangelical begins by sharing the gospel with those of his own culture, and eventually moves out to similar and even radically different cultures. He dwells on the words of Jesus: "You shall be My witnesses both in Jerusalem, and in all Judea and Samaria, and even to the remotest part of the earth" (Acts 1:8).

I suppose that everyone covets power of one kind or another, but the evangelical relates power to evangelism-missions. "You shall receive power," Jesus promised, "and you shall be My witnesses." The evangelical does not assume peculiar intellectual prowess, social prominence, or political superiority but that God will sustain him as he bears testimony to the gospel.

The decision called for is both easy and unimaginably difficult. It is easy because one need not turn from life in most of its conventional ways; it is desperately hard because it demands one's total allegiance to Christ. The undertaking is seen as a constant spiritual warfare, which demands that the Christian be adequately trained and continually alert.

Evangelism-missions is also a task that brings out the less noble and undisciplined character of those engaged in it. Being "desirous to insure a response to the Gospel, we have compromised our message, manipulated our hearers through pressure techniques, and become unduly preoccupied with statistics or even dishonest in our use of them."[13] All this speaks poorly of our motivation, let alone of the practice. Repentance must go hand in hand with evangelistic endeavor, lest in declaring the gospel to others, we ourselves become hard of hearing.

There is no more certain way to rally evangelicals than to announce the purpose of evangelism or extend it to the regions beyond. That is where the action is so far as the evangelical is concerned, not to the exclusion of other matters but at dead center.

READER'S SUMMARY

There remains to review those basic points which we have covered:

1. Missions is essentially evangelism viewed in global perspective. It portrays those who have received the good news taking it across cultural boundaries to those who have yet to hear. If anything, the evangelical is more interested in missions than evangelism as narrowly conceived. It seems to him that everyone should have the privilege of hearing the gospel once before we repeat the message over and over to the callous and indifferent.

2. Ralph Winter assisted us by distinguishing among E–1, E–2, and E–3 evangelism: where one shares with those in his own culture, bridges to a similar culture, or reaches to a radically different culture. The preference is

for E–1 evangelism, but we do not rule out the obligation to minister to those beyond the confines of our own culture.

3. The evangelical has assumed more than his share in pressing the claims of Christ in difficult surroundings. Time and again his blood paved the way for others who came in more leisurely fashion, without the same burden for the lost. He made mistakes, many of them in the process, but learned as a result and kept at the task.

4. "One may think of missions as a burden, a challenge, or an opportunity," we observed, while "the evangelical views it as something of a challenge *and* an opportunity." Each closed door seems to signal that another means to open. The evangelical comforts himself with the thought of God's sovereign purpose and the example of Christ. It always seems too soon to lay aside his active concern for missions.

5. This concern inevitably introduces the Christ and culture issue, how to relate the changeless gospel to varying contexts. The evangelical takes a both/and position: Christ and culture. He agrees with Brunner that "culture necessarily degenerates where it is made God." He believes that if we seek first the kingdom of God, the kingdoms of men may fall rightfully into place.

6. Perhaps 90 percent of what we think of as culture remains essentially intact after conversion. However, the evangelical anticipates that his faith will inevitably clash with custom at some points. He primes himself to withstand the pressure to conform at such junctures, while building common bonds at other points.

7. Where is the action for the evangelical? In evangelism-missions, where the good news is being shared, believed, and held as a sacred trust.

Part
III

THE EVANGELICAL CONSCIENCE

8

How Evangelicals View Themselves

How do evangelicals view themselves? The answer does not come easily or with certainty, but we shall at least make a proposal.

Several lines of thought suggest that evangelicals generally see themselves as a faithful remnant of orthodox Christianity in the modern age, a people of God set afloat in the sea of the Enlightenment.

We shall want to cast back upon the preceding generations of Christians to witness how self-perception may have differed and then pick up the theme of the evangelical as a remnant people. We shall consider history first and then analyze the situation.

In Retrospect

The first three centuries of Christianity, up to the time of Constantine, witnessed a remarkable spread of the faith. From a small, persecuted sect, Christianity emerged as the most promising contender for the allegiance of the ancient world. "It was because of what Jesus did to his intimates and because of their belief in him and in his death, resurrection, and early return that Christianity set out upon its career of conquest," reasons the noted church historian Kenneth Scott Latourette. "It was because, for some reason, these experiences and convictions persisted in succeeding generations that the faith possessed the inner dynamic which continued to give it driving power."[1] And so there existed a Messianic fellowship.

We today can never fully appreciate the unencumbered nature of the early Christian experience and we deceive ourselves by supposing otherwise. One did not have to look up the church directory to determine whether to worship in a Presbyterian, Pentecostal, or Roman Catholic church. There was an unrefined quality to the Christian community.

Our efforts to recover that pristine quality, such as calling for a New Testament church or rejecting the denominational designations, prove self-defeating. What results is simply another modern-day branch of the Christian faith and not the undifferentiated fellowship of the early centuries.

The point is that the early Christians were aware of their distinctive identity only as those who lived in the afterglow of the resurrection. The personal vindication of Jesus as Lord drew them into a fellowship of those of like precious faith, and cooperative ministry.

But well before Constantine a change was under way:

The memory of Christ "after the flesh" could hardly have survived the second century, if that long. In its place grew up an elaborate system of theology, employing Greek concepts for apologetic purposes, to which we give the term scholasticism. . . . The centrality of Jesus still persisted, but a hierarchial stress had replaced a historical one. It was no longer Jesus coming among men but Christ reigning through His Church, which governed biblical hermeneutics.[2]

So dawned the age of Christendom, or Constantinian Christianity, the peculiar wedding of Christian faith to the Western establishment.

Christendom fostered a majority feeling. "Before Constantine, the church had striven, by and large, to keep itself aloof from the world and so had left the latter undisturbed," perhaps as much from necessity as because of an ideal, but "beginning with Constantine, except for the more palpably antagonistic religious cults, it still allowed the world mostly to go on its own course, but it had now taken into its membership those who made up the world."[3] The church converted as it could and blessed the rest, so as to raise a sacred canopy over all of life.

I lived for several years in the section of South Boston called the Gate of Heaven parish. Not that I belonged to that particular church, but in predominantly Roman Catholic South Boston one did not have to do so in order to be designated by the parish district. This situation brings to mind the nature of a religious establishment such as existed in the Constantinian era. Others might be tolerated *as part of* the religious-social culture where Christianity reserved for itself the special privileges. There were, of course, those who disrupted the serenity of medieval Christendom, only to have order restored by persuasion or force, until the Reformation erupted in all its fury. Following this critical juncture, when the Reformers left their labors, the seventeenth-century Protestant scholastics pieced together an alternative to Roman Catholic Europe. It was sort of a Protestant Christendom, with church and state aligned along a different course. Consequently, the Roman Catholic and Protestant districts locked in ambitious competition and not uncommonly gave way to conflict as well.

Thereafter the Enlightenment intervened as a repudiation of Christendom in any form whatsoever. The Enlightenment declared itself emancipated and the emancipator. It thought itself to be the new David bent on slaying a Goliath church, a goal it pursued relentlessly.

Roman Catholicism resisted the attack of the Enlightenment more tenaciously and persistently than did Protestantism generally. It dug its trenches deeply, sometimes opposing the march of time as well as the error it brought with it.

Protestantism was more inclined to ride with the prevailing current, while at the same time attempting to preserve some of the more basic features of the faith. It lightened the theological burden as it went, so that eventually one had difficulty identifying the Christian cargo it professed to bear.

The modern evangelical movement grew out of these unsettled times, when the Roman Catholic community was feeling the increasingly impossible strain of resisting the winds of the time and Protestantism was having second thoughts about being so cooperative. Evangelicalism appeared as a remnant within the institutional church and even a smaller remnant among contemporary man. It had no broader ecclesiastical or cultural base on which to build.

The fact that evangelicalism has grown so extensively over the intervening years has not essentially altered the remnant psychology. The evangelical still sees himself as one of a company within the circle of the church and within the larger circle of the world.

In Relief

What might otherwise appear as unrelated characteristics of the evangelical movement cohere through the unifying remnant motif. For instance, Donald Bloesch comments on the trait of holiness: "Evangelical theology

holds that holiness in life is a fruit and evidence of justify-
ing faith. Personal holiness does not earn our salvation,
but it confirms and attests a salvation already received in
faith."[4] The evangelical acknowledges the Biblical injunction, "You shall consecrate yourselves therefore and
be holy, for I am the LORD your God" (Lev. 20:7). Like
Israel before her, the church qualifies as "a chosen race,
a royal priesthood, a holy nation, a people for God's own
possession" (I Peter 2:9).

We can perhaps best get at the evangelical perspective
on holiness by contrasting it with the monastic tradition.
The evangelical understands holiness to be the goal of all
rather than of a select few. Who, he wonders, would
desire to spend eternity with God, yet not want to cultivate God's fellowship in the present?

The second difference relates to the evangelical's seeing the holiness ideal as realized *in* the world and not
apart from it. J. Gresham Machen expressed the evangelical perspective: "Instead of obliterating the distinction between the Kingdom and the world, or on the other
hand withdrawing from the world into a sort of intellectual monasticism, let us go forth joyfully, enthusiastically,
to make the world subject to God."[5] This attitude seems
more proper to the evangelical than the monastic alternative.

The evangelical has come to his remnant perception in
part as an appeal to Scripture but also from the exigencies
of history. He acted in accordance with his understanding
of Biblical teaching and reacted to the uncompromising
demands of the Enlightenment. The results have been
predictably mixed, some good and some bad, and they all
will become more understandable as we keep the remnant
clue before us.

The evangelical stress on Christ's return is a second

characteristic that seems unrelated to anything else until
the remnant motif ties it into the larger perspective.
Ernest Sandeen singles out the dispensational element in
the evangelical movement as holding

an intensely pessimistic view of the world's future combined
with a hope in God's imminent and direct intervention in
human life. God established covenants which have always been
broken by virtually all men involved in them. God waited,
restraining judgment, but eventually punished the disobedient
while saving just men such as Noah, Joshua, or Ezra. This
pattern of past events was projected into the future through the
interpretation of prophecy.[6]

Probably to characterize the evangelical as "intensely pessimistic" would be too strong a statement. He is a pessimistic optimist or an optimistic pessimist. He sees the
times as always as bright as God's presence and as dismal
as man's intractability.

In any case, the evangelical views mankind in violation
of God's covenant provisions. The disobedient masses
pride themselves in the incidental things that should be
taken for granted and leave undone the greater require-
ments of God's law. They pick their way through life as
if there would never be a time for accurate accounting.

So also the evangelical thinks of God as remarkably
patient with his erring creatures. "The Lord is not slow
about His promise, as some count slowness, but is patient
toward you, not wishing for any to perish but for all to
come to repentance" (II Peter 3:9). The great sufferings
of the world are less cause to question God's love than to
accent his compassionate endurance.

Still God never leaves himself without a witness. We
may discover a remnant of the faithful throughout history, such as Simeon, a man "righteous and devout," who

looked "for the consolation of Israel" (Luke 2:25); those whose confidence rested in God's promises, whose faith resisted the temptation to join with the complacently religious, and whose hope in the ultimate reign of God remained steadfast.

We have seen in select instances how the remnant motif unifies certain evangelical traits. It is not a simple clue, or equally applicable to all cases, but a helpful guide to a better understanding of the evangelical movement.

REMNANT DYNAMICS

We move now to consider how the remnant concept works out in practice. In the first place, remnant awareness permits the evangelical to take an unconventional stand. He resembles the resolute prophet Ezekiel when he declared: "So My hand will be against the prophets who see false visions and utter lying divinations. They will have no place in the council of My people" (Ezek. 13:9). The populace anticipated encouraging tidings and the false prophets gave them what they desired, while Ezekiel stood alone in protest.

No one finds it easy to break ranks, but it is easier for the evangelical because of his remnant perspective. He braces himself for the moment when he must confess, "Here I stand, God helping me, I can do no less."

Only the emotionally sick welcome such experiences and delight in the pain they bring. But the evangelical would rather accept such trying moments with resolute devotion than buy a costly compromise with the world.

An illustration may help to reinforce the point. One day in class at the university a snide remark was passed concerning the evangelist Billy Graham. The professor, known to hold the evangelical position in contempt, nevertheless stopped the perpetrator of the comment with a withering gaze. "I suppose you mean to be humorous," he began, "but the fact is that if you put someone like that in a new surrounding, he would make his convictions felt." The laughter had disappeared as the instructor continued, "And those of our persuasion would blend into the background."

The remnant psychology also provides a sense of intimacy, with God primarily but with others as well. God is real to the evangelical, not always equally real and not as real for some as for others, but predictably real in any case. Billy Graham speaks out for the evangelical experience: "When we covet His Presence more than any earthly possession, He favors us by filling the vacuum of our hearts with His fullness."[7] One of Graham's often-repeated remarks is to the effect that God could not be dead because "I talked with him this morning." Now, one can laugh over that comment and discredit it all one wants, but it accurately reflects the evangelical's sensitivity to the presence of God.

The evangelical family has been, at least in the past, a rather closely knit one. Everyone seemed to know a mutual acquaintance, if not personally, then at least by reputation. It is as though an inner circle of like spirits were bustling about in the Lord's service, waving to one another and keeping to their several tasks.

Stories also make their rounds. They are told and retold as evangelical haggada.[8] They pick up variations along the way and sometimes find their way into print, strengthening that sense of evangelical intimacy.

Evangelicals have often been a struggling minority (although less so today than formerly), perhaps with no church to call their own, little social prestige, and often considered to be religious fanatics. The advent of gospel broadcasting has been one of the sources of encouragement along the way. The evangelical turned on the "Old Fashioned Revival Hour" to pick up the familiar strains of gospel music, the fatherly voice of the radio preacher, and the response of men and women to the invitation. (He might, as a friend of mine did, turn up the volume so others could not help hearing the declaration of the gospel.) This was the family hour, the evangelical family hour.

Finally, the most important remnant dynamic is embodied in Jesus' words to his disciples: "You are the salt of the earth" (Matt. 5:13). In order to retain this saltiness and to gain respect as a divine catalyst, the evangelical must first come to appreciate his own distinctive identity.

Bernard Ramm protests the similarity between much "pop evangelical prophetic literature" and "cultic eschatology." "When a cultic mentality is so apparent in evangelical literature, it is also apparent that many evangelicals have lost the sense of the inner structure of evangelical literature."[9] They have lost the reality of what it means to be an evangelical. And they have ceased to be an effective catalyst.

To correct this situation the evangelical must reestablish his roots in Scripture. He has to get back to the fountainhead of his faith, to weigh seriously the meaning and significance of Holy Writ.

The evangelical must also delve into his own peculiar heritage. He needs to retrace the route by which evangelicalism has come to the present day. He must consider the reason for each turn along the way and its current pertinence.[10]

The evangelical will likewise come to understand the world around him if he is to fulfill his catalyst function. Theology is never done in a vacuum, nor should it be understood in one. Whether we think of Biblical or systematic theology, the premise holds true.

The world does not need broad generalities or pat answers. To be a true catalyst, the evangelical must learn to apply sensitively the abiding truths of Scripture to genuine needs at hand. And this requires that we become students of the world in which we live. We need to add the daily newspaper to our Biblical curriculum.

In this chapter we have attempted to understand the evangelical psyche. "To describe an evangelical is to describe a state of mind, a religious posture, a way of looking at spiritual reality," Killian McDonnell concludes.[11] McDonnell may overlook something of the doctrinal thrust that evangelicals hold in common, but he is correct in observing that there is an evangelical psyche at work, and it remains a significant element in our effort to understand the evangelical movement.

READER'S SUMMARY

Here let us draw our findings together into a sharper focus:

1. It seems that the evangelical self-perception resembles that of a latter-day remnant. Previously, Christendom had fostered a majority feeling. Those who deviated from Christianity were considered to be non-Christians, exceptions to the norm. The Reformation replaced the Catholic with a Protestant establishment, while the Enlightenment challenged any Christian establishment and eventually undercut its influence. "The modern evangelical movement grew out of such unsettled times" (when the Roman Catholic community was feeling the increasingly impossible strain of resisting the winds of the time and Protestantism was having second thoughts about its

cooperation with them) as "a people of God set afloat in the sea of the Enlightenment."

2. This remnant theme helps us appreciate what might otherwise appear as unrelated characteristics of the evangelical movement. It ties together such predictable emphases as those on holiness and the second advent, to mention but two.

3. The remnant mind-set enables the evangelical to take a vigorous stand in the face of opposition. He can remain resolute when others seem swept away by some shift in current. Not that he finds such an experience easy, but it is by the grace of God tolerable.

4. This perspective also contributes a sense of intimacy with God and those of like evangelical faith. It generates a peculiar certainty, so that the evangelical does not feel abandoned to some oppressive task. It accounts for what an earlier generation of preachers called "the glory road."

5. Finally, the evangelical sees himself as a catalyst in life. He thinks of being the salt of the earth and light of the world. He may not be a very significant ingredient as such, but God has a way of honoring his feeble efforts.

6. In striving to be the best possible catalyst, the evangelical must renew his strength by drawing upon the Scriptures and becoming better aware of the world to which he ministers. He grasps the Bible in one hand and the newspaper in the other, so that he can perceptively apply abiding truths to the needs at hand.

7. The evangelical movement includes theoretical considerations and relevant actions, but it is also a state of mind or psyche. We cannot hope to understand the evangelical apart from that self-perception which permits him to function as he does.

9

In Regard to Ecumenical Concerns

Evangelicals feel various obligations growing out of their role as a faithful remnant. The first that we shall discuss is their sense of ecumenical responsibility.

While the term "ecumenical" suggests the universal nature of the church, it has come to mean the quest for Christian unity. "I do not ask in behalf of these alone," Jesus prayed, "but for those also who believe in Me through their word; that they may all be one" (John 17:20–21). The evangelical takes this concern to heart.

A Point of View

The evangelical insists that organizational utility should not be singled out as the sole ecumenical concern. "When the mourners gathered at the grave of Lazarus, they experienced perfect unity," Edward John Carnell reminisces. "Jesus Himself was the rallying point for fellowship, doctrine, and form: *fellowship* because the mourners were bound by cords of love; *doctrine* because the teaching of the Lord was normative; and *form* because the will of the Lord became the will of the group."[1] The evangelical holds that the ecumenical endeavor must accent fellowship and doctrine as well as form or organization.

Fellowship is a critical factor and an appropriate consideration. "Behold, how good and how pleasant it is for brothers to dwell together in unity!" (Ps. 133:1). The evangelical approves, fosters, and commends these sentiments to others. At the same time, he resists those forces which are detrimental to Christian fellowship—for instance, when self-seeking is rationalized as contending for the faith or belligerence masquerades as zeal.

Scripture reminds us that faith is also a vital concern. The early believers "were continually devoting themselves to the apostles' teaching and to fellowship" (Acts 2:42). They took Biblical instruction seriously, not as some passing interest but in order to reach a persisting goal.

"To be truly biblical is one of the most difficult achievements," Bernard Ramm warns. "We are always under pressures to see the Scriptures in other than their true meaning."[2] The evangelical urges that we not take matters of belief for granted. Each generation must carefully review the meaning and significance of its faith for the time in which it lives.

The evangelical's critics fault him for allowing his concern for faith to violate fellowship, but he cannot assume one to the exclusion of the other. Belief provides the basis for fellowship.

So also form without genuine faith would be meaningless. "Unity is not contingent on organization," J. Marcellus Kik argues, "but on union with Christ."[3] The evangelical reminds himself that Jesus selectively prayed "for those who believe in Me" through the apostles' teaching.

Faith and fellowship will require some form of expression. Thus we read of the early company of believers holding things in common, frequenting the Temple precincts, and sharing their meals together. The apostles provided the required leadership until the burdens became too heavy; then some of the duties were delegated to others. All this suggests a flexible, adaptive community that met the needs at hand rather than perpetuating form for its own sake.

While the evangelical pursues the ecumenical ideal by way of keeping faith, fellowship, and form in focus, he often appears to be dragging his feet. It seems to some of those looking on that he not only lacks enthusiasm for the ecumenical endeavor, but actually provides opposition. Vernon Grounds means to correct this false impression by distinguishing his evangelical position from the schismatic. The schismatic "disfranchises all denominations and sects but his own. He holds that people who belong to any other fellowship are at best second-class citizens of the Kingdom of God, if, in fact, they belong to the kingdom."[4]

"But this has not been the mainstream of our evangelical witness," Grounds correctly hastens to add. The evangelical has seldom doubted, even for the moment, that there were genuine Christians in folds other than his own.

The schismatic likewise holds that every doctrine is pretty much on a par with every other doctrine. "Since everything in the Bible is equally true, everything in the Bible, he argues, must be equally significant. The fact that Paul left a cloak at Troas is as vital as the fact that Jesus Christ shed his blood as an atonement for our sins."[5] To deviate in one's interpretation at the one point is as serious as at the other.

The schismatic perpetrates this hoax in the name of Scripture, but that is precisely the place where he makes his mistake. It is this narrow sectarian spirit that Paul condemns in his letter to Corinth: the tendency to draw the line so exactly as to exclude those who differ on some secondary emphasis.

In the final instance, the schismatic "holds aloof from all other believers, viewing them with lordly disdain, unconcealed contempt, and downright ill-will. Any fellow-believer who makes an effort to promote evangelical ecumenicity, the schismatic is likely to denounce as an agent of satanic darkness."[6] The tragedy of Christian disunity does not pain him in the least.

The evangelical contrasts at all these points. He assumes no monopoly on faith, sustains a distinction between the more or less critical doctrines (as well as a margin of error even as concerns the basic fundamentals), and grieves over the lack of unity he experiences within the Christian fellowship. He strives to keep faith, fellowship, and form in proper balance.

IN HISTORICAL PERSPECTIVE

We might profitably put this evangelical approach into historical perspective. Earle Cairns identifies three eras as they relate to the ecumenical quest: unity by expulsion (to A.D. 380), unity by coercion (380–1648), and from denominational pluralism to ecumenism (1648 forward).[7] Cairns points out how heresy and division threatened both the doctrinal and the structural unity of the early church. Ignatius represents the ecumenical attack taken as a result. The bishop of Antioch wrote several letters to churches in Asia during the early part of the second century. Congregations, he affirmed, must be in harmony with the church hierarchy, who through apostolic succession were in harmony with Christ. This would create a blameless unity and permit them to be "partakers of God always."[8]

Ignatius held that apart from democratically selected and divinely appointed men there could be no universal church.[9] He further warned that schismatics would forfeit their inheritance in the kingdom of God.[10] He intended to persuade when possible and excommunicate if necessary.

This earliest period surrendered to an established church supported by temporal authorities. "The voluntary association of oneself with the church gave way to birth into the *universal* church and compulsory allegiance on pain both of spiritual and temporal penalties."[11] To unity by expulsion was added unity by compulsion.

The relentless ecumenical drive introduced new and unprecedented struggles for leadership in the church. Where individual heretics had been previously eliminated, now entire dissenting groups were forced out. Those remaining had to surrender their differences, even when in violation of conscience.

Such an inflexible spirit contributed to the eventual division between Eastern and Western churches and subsequently to the Reformation. The latter retained the idea of compulsion, applying it now within the particular national church. While the Anabaptists protested this oppressive link between church and state, they had little overall effect on the prevailing situation.

It was not until the close of the Thirty Years' War in 1648 that an increased measure of religious toleration came about, and with it a time when ecumenism became genuinely optional. There were early efforts such as that of Zinzendorf, bishop of the Moravian Church, who tried unsuccessfully to bring about a union of the Pietist and Lutheran movements. The Lutheran George Calixtus, Arminian Hugo Grotius, and educator John Amos Comenius of the Bohemian Brethren were also among those who had made proposals to achieve greater unity.

The nineteenth century witnessed increased ecumenical activity, especially along the line of cooperative agencies for furthering evangelistic, missionary, and educational goals. It spawned the American Board of Commissioners for Foreign Missions (1810), the American Sunday School Union (1824), the YMCA (1851), Christian Endeavor (1881), the Student Volunteer Movement (1886), and the World's Student Christian Federation (1895). It also resulted in a closer liaison among existing bodies.

The ecumenical spirit leaped boldly into the twentieth century. There were the intraconfessional confederations, beginning with the Anglicans (1847), and embracing the Reformed (1875), Methodists (1881), Congregationalists (1891), Baptists (1905), and Lutherans (1923). The interconfessional efforts also proliferated. The International Missionary Council (1921) would eventually merge with the World Council of Churches (1961). The latter came into being in 1948 and held periodic conferences thereafter. The Open and Institutional Church League (1894), the National Federation of Churches and Christian Workers (1901), and the Federal Council of the Churches of Christ in America (1908) were social action centered in their orientation. The conservative American Council of Christian Churches (1941) and the National Association of Evangelicals (1943) attempted to set forth more adequate doctrinal planks for cooperative venture.

The council of churches movement (federal and world) assumed a federation structure. While allowing the possibility of something more organic to develop, it denied the charge of building a "superchurch." An abbreviated creed, generally lacking in definition, allowed for a broadly inclusive membership.

There have been a number of instances of organic union. The Church of Scotland (1929), The United Presbyterian Church in the U.S.A. (1958), The Methodist Church (1939), the United Church of Canada (1925), and the Church of South India (1947) are examples of intraconfessional and interconfessional mergers.

However, neither the council of churches nor organic unions seem to be doing well at the moment. The council of churches, plagued by dissension and disinterest, has cut back all along the line. The efforts toward organic union also bogged down, their energy drained by splinter groups, declining membership, and uncertain loyalties.

A NEW LIBERTY

That is not to say that the ecumenical spirit has necessarily decreased, but it appears to be taking a less formal and more functional direction. Christians have discovered a new liberty in associating together in Bible clubs, evangelistic activity, and specific ministries. They are weary of the round of committee meetings and accommodations that provide very little tangible results.

I remember a discussion with a man who for some years had been active in ecumenical concerns. Time had taken a toll on his idealism and pretty well deleted his earlier enthusiasm. He seemed a bit surprised that I taught at a nondenominational Christian school. After thoughtfully weighing my related comments, he concluded that my experience was a better example of ecumenism than the parade of committee meetings and negotiations that demanded his attention.

"The resurgence of evangelicalism can have favorable ecumenical implications, even though evangelicals are noted for their biting criticisms of the organized ecumenical movement. They remind us that church union can never be achieved on a political or sociological basis but only on one that is theological."[12] Not to point out the failures alone, the evangelical resurgence highlights the ingredients required for success with the ecumenical endeavor.

For instance, the characteristic evangelical emphasis on evangelism and missions has ecumenical implications. It calls together those who respond to their Lord's commission to make disciples of all nations.

Social concern does not nourish the ecumenical spirit in the same way. The evangelistic task is distinctive to the Christian community, while social concern is shared with others.

The evangelical has an ecumenical conscience. Were that not so, he would find it easier simply to ignore the whole issue. He walks the path between schismatic and conventionalist (one who uncritically accepts the religious *status quo*). He cannot accept the presumption of the schismatic or the complacency of the conventionalist.

The schismatic, it bears repeating, assumes a monopoly on truth, that doctrines are of essentially equal importance, and that divisions should be of little cause for concern. The conventionalist implies that truth is relative, that doctrine is of little consequence, and presses for indiscriminate union. The evangelical ground lies between the two positions, making any given step a bit uncertain, almost assured to bring criticism from schismatic and conventionalist alike.

Perhaps I may speak from personal experience. It concerns a pastorate I served within a theologically inclusive old-line denomination. A schismatic friend accosted me with the pointed comment, "If you lie down with dogs, you will get up with fleas." Conversely, a denominational official told me that I would never "amount to anything" in the denomination because of my misgivings with the current ecumenical movement. I suspect that the evangelical must expect fire from both sides if his ecumenical conscience is functioning properly.

The evangelical's conscience alerts him to an ecumenical ideal. It warns him against contrived solutions to Christian disunity, while encouraging him to exercise the full privilege and responsibility of membership in the community of faith.

READER'S SUMMARY

We do well to sum up this first inquiry into the evangelical conscience:

1. The evangelical is uneasy with any superficial approach to the ecumenical endeavor. He reasons that belief, fellowship, and form are all legitimate considerations in what often appears as an illusive goal.

2. The evangelical stresses the importance of doctrine. Faith lies at the basis of fellowship and provides the rationale for ecclesiastical structure.

3. Fellowship likewise receives attention. The evangelical decries the kind of belligerence that masquerades as zeal, and the self-seeking rationalized as contending for the faith. He concurs with the sentiment that it is good for brothers to dwell together in unity.

4. Thus he seeks out an appropriate organic expression. "A flexible, adaptive organization," we concluded, "that would meet the needs at hand" rather than force some stifling conformity out of anxiety to present a common front.

5. The evangelical assumes no monopoly on faith, sustains a distinction between primary and secondary beliefs,

and grieves over the disunity he experiences within the Christian fellowship. He repudiates any compromise of conviction or the partisan spirit that sows discord.

6. He recalls that the ecumenical cause was carried under threat of expulsion, then coercion, and more recently persuasion. History seems to him to caution restraint when we take too uncritical an approach to ecumenism and to encourage us in the pursuit of unity when interest wanes.

10

In Regard to Social Action

There is a renewal of social awareness among many in the evangelical camp. As Earle Cairns points out, "Contemporary Evangelicals, who for a time ignored their responsibility as Christians in Society, are becoming increasingly aware that . . . [they] have a responsibility to put the principles of Christ into action . . . in the social order in which they live."[1]

If this is a genuine renewal, why did evangelicals lose their zeal for social action in the first place? We shall not have to look far for the answer.

A STEP BACKWARD

"During its long history orthodox or conservative, Christianity had stressed the application of its message to social ills," Millard Erickson explains. "In the nineteenth century, for example, evangelicals in America were in the forefront of the forces contending for the abolition of slavery. As the twentieth century moved on, however, fundamentalism neglected this emphasis."[2] The evangelical heritage of social concern diminished as fundamentalism struggled to sustain the essentials of the Christian faith.

Although we do not mean to excuse the fundamentalist's withdrawal from social action, there are considerations that help us to appreciate his dilemma better. In the first place, the fundamentalist reacted against the unrealistic idealism of the time. He appreciated, as few of his contemporaries did, the radical nature of sin. He repeatedly worried against treating symptoms as the source of the difficulty.

We should also note the extreme drain of energy from the fundamentalism/modernist controversy. The fundamentalist felt that the very future of the Christian faith was at stake and gave the conflict his virtually unqualified attention. Had there been less significance to the outcome or had the enemy been less formidable, the fundamentalist's record on social ethics might have been considerably better.[3]

Moreover, the fundamentalists contributed selectively to the social effort. This was especially true where it would not appear to compromise their conviction.

The stereotype born of polemics does us disservice at this point. The fundamentalist portrayed the modernist as a "do-gooder," filled with pious platitudes and out of touch with reality. The modernist, in turn, likened the fundamentalist to the priest and the Levite who skirted a man fallen by the Jericho road. Both appraisals had an element of truth in them but failed to give a balanced view of either side.

When all the proper qualifications have been noted, we are left with what Carl F. H. Henry describes as "the uneasy conscience of modern fundamentalism." The problems of racial intolerance, exploitation of labor, and prison conditions were left largely unresolved, and the great reservoir of Biblical truth and Christian compassion all too little tapped.

Moving Ahead

Carl Henry alleges that the Christian task force today is divided concerning what attack to take on social conditions. Shall we stress the spiritual regeneration of persons, without which our social gains will eventually flounder? Or shall we rely on legislation and social action as the necessary means of managing complex social problems? The question touches us at practically every turn. "It is involved in one's attitude . . . toward the crusade for civil rights and for racial integration," Henry observes. "It is involved in the debate over government and public welfare."[4]

Henry outlines four strategies available to the contemporary evangelical: revolution, reform, revaluation, and regeneration. And he defines them in order:

By *revolution* we mean the radical change of social patterns, in their essential constitution, through violence and compulsion. By *reformation* we mean that gradual but pervasive ethical amendment of particular abuses which secures a decisive improvement of prevailing social character and forms. By *revaluation* we mean a fresh intellectual comprehension and direction, whereby social life and structures are critically reassessed in the light of transcendent moral norms. By *regeneration* we mean transformation by supernatural impulse in individual lives whereby the social scene is renewed through a divine spiritual motivation.[5]

While it appears that we have four social strategies to select from, there are actually two—regeneration and revolution. The remaining alternatives play a complementary role regardless of the direction we take.

"All those who take up the sword," Jesus warned, "shall perish by the sword" (Matt. 26:52). Just what is the problem with the revolutional strategy regarding social action? Revolution, in the first place, presumes too much. Its advocates deceive themselves with the idea that their perception is so far superior to that of the persons they mean to depose as to justify the inevitable *excess* involved in revolution. They leave off being men in order to play at being gods. Crusades drink deeply of such intoxicating presumption, and pity the victims of their drunken fantasy!

Revolution thus takes an unconscionable toll. We can live more readily with a degree of injustice than pay the cost of overthrowing the order that brings us mixed benefits.

Revolution also offers too little. What is left in the wake of revolution? Deep wounds (difficult if not impossible to heal), lost values, and uncertain rewards. The new system provides neither panacea nor the promise of permanence. Our difficulties reincarnate in novel forms.

Regeneration as a social strategy appears to be more promising. It rightly stresses the need for personal commitment if we are to achieve permanent change. Otherwise, social progress erodes against the unrelenting resistance of those involved.

Regeneration also allows important roles for reformation and evaluation, both to pave the way for commitment and to implement it thereafter. The three seem to be natural allies in constructive social endeavor.

Finally, regeneration may even incorporate revolution in more extreme instances. It does so hesitantly, while weighing the danger involved. But there are occasions where we must at least consider revolution (not as the dominant approach to social need, but as a limited means within a larger strategy).

Regeneration appeals to the evangelical as the preferred alternative to social action, as we shall see in turning through the pages of history.

EVANGELICAL HERITAGE

"What motives would cause a man such as Zachary to devote his time to the cause of the abolition of slavery to the point that his fortunes, entrusted to others, were endangered and even lost? What would cause Shaftesbury to serve for fifty-seven out of sixty years in public service without any remuneration and lead him to sell valued family portraits to raise money to improve the homes on the estates which he had inherited from his father?"[6] What motivates men to act in such a self-effacing fashion and on behalf of others? We cannot speak for all men, but the experience of these men ran a course much like that of William Wilberforce. In 1784, the latter became painfully conscious of his sinfulness and lost condition while reading together with Isaac Milner in Philip Doddridge's *The Rise and Progress of Religion in the Soul.* The following year the two of them undertook to read the Greek New Testament to confirm or to raise questions as to the credibility of Doddridge's claims. As a result, Wilberforce came under a deep sense of conviction, and in December of 1785 he made his peace with God.

"For most of his contemporaries, religion was primarily an ethical matter, and salvation merely involved attendance at the services of the church and other religious activities," Cairns explains. "This view clashed with Wilberforce's new conviction that 'the renovation of our corrupted nature' and 'the attainment of every Christian grace' could come alone through faith in the work of Christ for us."[7] He had come to understand the evangelical character of the Christian faith and to act upon it.

Wilberforce now sought out the will of God for his life; it seemed to direct him to take up the abolition cause. He would eventually report that being the instrument of eliminating the slave trade and opening India to the gospel were the greatest moments in his ministry. "Wilberforce's labors on behalf of the black slaves had their origin in his experience of conversion, which drew out his heart in love to God, and had their motivation in the consequent love of man."[8]

"You shall love the Lord your God with all your heart, and with all your soul, and with all your mind," Jesus summarized the law, and "you shall love your neighbor as yourself" (Matt. 22:37, 39). Such was Wilberforce's experience with the grace of God on the way to serve his fellowman.

The evangelicals of Wilberforce's character also reflected a predictable strategy when it came to bringing their conviction to bear on social institutions. "They all had a healthy respect for the power of truth based on facts to mold a public opinion that would force action."[9] They were not what we negatively imply by the term "manipulators." They did not trick people, nor force them, but built up such an impressive case that public opinion rallied behind their cause.

When Wilberforce managed to get a select committee of the House of Commons to examine evidence concerning the slave trade, Thomas Clarkson provided most of the needed evidence. Clarkson had been informed of a sailor who had firsthand experience of how the slaves were procured, but he did not know his name or the ship on which he sailed. Realizing the importance of the information, Clarkson set out to discover the man. He boarded 160 vessels at Deptford, 60 at Woolwich, Sheeness, and

Chatham and 40 at Plymouth. The 317th ship, the *Melampus*, anchoring at Plymouth, delivered the informant at long last and a critical link was forged in the case against slavery.

The evangelical cannot salve his social conscience by an occasional fling at some iniquity. He must assume the burden of evidence.

So also must he publicize the facts. George Stephen formed The Agency Committee to arrange for public meetings to disperse information on slavery and further petitions for its abolition. Wilberforce and others wrote letters to the editor of *The Times*, erected billboards to stimulate interest, and addressed the annual public meetings of the missionary societies. Cowper's poem "The Slave's Complaint" added to the impetus. (It was first circulated in fashionable circles and later set to music and became a popular ballad.) Josiah Wedgwood created fine china portraying a kneeling black man with hands clasped and upraised, along with the words, "Am I not a man and a brother?" Pamphlets were used widely. There were boycotts of slave-grown products. (Clarkson alleged that in 1792 some 300,000 stopped using sugar produced in the British West Indies.) The abolitionists also published the *Christian Observer* and *The Anti-Slavery Reporter*. Such were some of the varied means used to get their message before the public.

These evangelicals bathed their efforts in prayer. "This consideration of the techniques by which the evangelicals brought faith, love and hope to bear on the problems of society shows that they did not substitute spirituality or oratory for self-sacrificing hard work in order to have authenticated facts to support their case," Cairns sums up. "They used every possible legitimate means to educate the public, especially the Christian public of En-

gland, in order to create a Christian public opinion. Then
by the vote, resolution and petitions, and by speeches by
leaders in Parliament, they focused this public opinion on
the issues so as to secure necessary legislation to correct
the evil. All these endeavors were undergirded by
prayer."[10] Thus evangelical action draws upon a life in
communion with God.

The evangelical does not view conversion as the conclusion to something but as its beginning. He must then
inquire into the purposes that God has for his life and this
is not limited to evangelism but reaches out to embrace
humankind in all their social needs. "What we should
seek for today is a social evangelicalism over an exclusively
individualistic evangelicalism," Donald Bloesch concludes. "Such a position will not deny the priority of
personal salvation but will seek to relate this to the nur-
ture and fellowship of the church and to the areas of
service in the world."[11] It will restore the evangelical
movement to its earlier course and good conscience.

A BALANCE

"The evangelical of today thinks of himself as conservative at many points, because he believes that the values
of faith and life are worth conserving," Sherwood Wirt
states the resulting dilemma. "At the same time he
refuses to turn into a tool in the hands of oppression and
privilege."[12] The hyperactivist faults him for an alleged
irrelevance; the vested interestes caution him against radical tendencies. Neither allows the socially conscious
evangelical a clear road to responsible action.

It seems to the evangelical that one group of his critics
repudiate the past. They shake the dust from their feet
in a futile effort to dislodge any reminder of what has

transpired. As a result, they become trapped by the limited perspective of the times.

Others seem to worship yesterday. Like programmed creatures destined to continue now meaningless behavior, they suppose that antiquity provides its own justification.

The evangelical rejects both options in favor of adapting our heritage to changing circumstances. He is concerned with our historical legacy, supposing that what men have labored for with such dedication should not be lightly weighed by posterity. For him "Christianity is one and not many and is not capable of continuous radical reinterpretation."[13] There must be a common understanding running throughout—what we have termed "Christian orthodoxy."

The evangelical greets any radical departure from historic Christian faith with suspicion, if not forthright opposition. For instance, the Jehovah's Witnesses' claim to recover a Biblical faith (distorted these many centuries by the church) triggers a built-in evangelical protest. Why should we suppose that they or anyone else can come up with some radical reinterpretation?

The Christian faith appears to the evangelical as a stream flowing from its source in Christ. There may be a twist in its course now and then, some historical eddy, a curious diversion, but it remains essentially unaltered in its course.

The evangelical thus shakes off the suggestion that Jesus was God's provision for a past era of history and that another is to be substituted for the present time. He likes to repeat the words "Jesus Christ is the same yesterday and today, yes and forever" (Heb. 13:8) as if to assure his hearers of the continuing relevance of the historic faith.

This is a delicate balance the evangelical strives to maintain but a necessary one. An uncritical appeal to the past offers no alternative and neither does novelty for its own sake. The evangelical means to bring abiding truth to bear on changing circumstances.

It follows that "Biblical revelation confines itself largely to ideal principles of social order; it does not commit itself to particular parties or programs of social reform."[14] The Christian is committed to justice but there are many different proposals and means for achieving that end. Christians may find themselves on different sides of a given issue and pressing some partisan perspective.

The evangelical sees nothing inconsistent with this lack of uniformity. He knows that he cannot give the endorsement of the church as a whole to a particular point of view. Nevertheless, he would like to demonstrate a concern for social issues within a somewhat predictable range of responses.

The evangelical, like the prophets before him, sees man's social needs primarily within a religious context. "Do two men walk together unless they have made an appointment [agreement]?" (Amos 3:3). How shall we expect to manage in God's world without respect for his will? There is no ultimate social solution that leaves God out of the picture.

Nor can there be disinterest in social matters when we take God into consideration. "If some one says, 'I love God,' and hates his brother, he is a liar; for the one who does not love his brother whom he has seen, cannot love God whom he has not seen. And this commandment we have from Him, that the one who loves God should love his brother also" (I John 4:20–21). Thus, while the evangelical social conscience suffered as a result of the fundamentalist/modernist controversy, it has shown new life of late. "A sense of social responsibility, buried too long, perhaps, under the wrong kind of conservative instincts, is rising to the surface and demanding a place in the sun," Wirt concludes. "People who accept the authority of the Bible are beginning to outgrow a limited approach to the basic social problems of twentieth-century living."[15]

READER'S SUMMARY

We review this further contact with the evangelical conscience:

1. The evangelical is experiencing a renewed concern for social action. While he accepts the responsibility of proclaiming the gospel, he does not take this as an excuse to ignore the extended needs of society.

2. The evangelical views social action as a return to historic Christian orthodoxy and as a recovery from the distortion that resulted from the fundamentalist/modernist controversy. He rejoices that a persisting concern for man in his social situation has surfaced once more.

3. Regeneration appeals to the evangelical as the best of social strategies. While willing to allow the other options to complement regeneration, he faults any effort that falls short of altering man's basic disposition.

4. The past illustrates the evangelical preference, as in the case of Wilberforce and his associates in their struggle against slavery. They were motivated out of Christian commitment to gather the necessary evidence, publicize the facts, and press for a decisive action.

5. There too we sensed how the evangelical tries to keep the past in gear with the present. He searches for a middle ground between the uncritical support of the *status quo* and radicalism for its own sake. He looks for opportunities to use that which is valuable in our legacy to serve this present age.

6. The evangelical is not unmindful of the limited goals that may be achieved from any course of social action, but this does not keep him from joining with men of goodwill in a venture that promises to ease man's burden and make life more inviting.

11

In the Political Arena

We have traced the evangelical conscience from its concerns with the church, through social action, and now to the political arena. More evangelicals are running for public office, actively supporting the individuals who seem to be the better candidates, and cooperating with those elected.

THE MANDATE

The evangelical naturally turns to Scripture as the foundation of his political endeavor. "Let every person be in subjection to the governing authorities. For there is no authority except from God, and those which exist are established by God. Therefore he who resists authority has opposed the ordinance of God; and they who have opposed will receive condemnation upon themselves" (Rom. 13:1–2). The apostle thus introduces a political dimension to discipleship, which we can trace throughout the Biblical narrative.

"Political considerations form a significant part of the Old Testament, preceding the monarchy and continuing into the return from captivity."[1] We likely have an indication of the clan arrangement in the early lists of Adam's descendants (Gen., ch. 5), reminding us how the extended family adjusted to manage public affairs. They were organized to legislate, enforce, and justify regulations that were thought to be advantageous to the group.

Moses, in turn, found the burden of judging Israel too great and appointed lesser magistrates to be trained in administering justice (Ex. 18:13–26). Thus he attempted to cope with the increasing political burden created by an expanding society.

The settlement of Canaan raised new difficulties for the people of Israel and they had no central authority to serve them. "In those days there was no king in Israel," the reporter laments; "everyone did what was right in his own eyes" (Judg. 21:25). A series of Hebrew champions (judges) not only eased the oppression from alien inhabitants of the land but brought limited order out of the chaotic situation. Eventually a prominent figure named Samuel came forward and was recognized from Dan to Beer-sheba as a man chosen by God for his office (I Sam. 3:10 to 4:1), and when he could no longer maintain his rigorous responsibilities, he appointed his sons to judge over Israel.

Samuel's successors served poorly, and so the elders petitioned Samuel to anoint a king over the nation. Samuel was reluctant, for he "saw in the request not simply a plea for better government but an escape from responsible rule, and interpreted it as a rejection of God. The representatives confirmed the fear by urging that the king usurp authority and prerogatives after the fashion of the pagan nations about them."[2]

The monarchy was short-lived; it soon broke into northern and southern kingdoms. Israel's road was pretty much downhill all the way and ended with captivity to Assyria. Judah fared better but eventually succumbed to Babylon. The victors consolidated their gains by resettlement, but when the situation eased, a series of Jewish migrations began under Cyrus.

While the fortunes of Israel varied, Jewish society never totally lacked a political reality. Its family structure contributed along with local councils of elders.

The Messiah inherited the political legacy of Israel. "Jesus lived in a religious establishment where practically his every move had political significance."[3] There was no separation of state and religion as we have experienced in the contemporary era.

The earliest Christians were Jews who drew upon both Jesus' instruction and then Jewish political experience. No doubt much of their perspective carried over as the fellowship became more diversified.

The Christian community lived an uneasy existence from the beginning. Its leaders were reprimanded and the congregations eventually persecuted. The Romans seem to have viewed the Christians at first as a harmless Jewish sect and then as an especially troublesome one. There was little opportunity for the believers to become part of the power structure, whether Jewish or Roman.

It was against such a background that the apostle enjoined his readers to obey the authorities as ordained of God. This should not be understood as compliance with any and all demands, regardless of how they impinge on conscience. "Then render to Caesar the things that are Caesar's," Jesus put the matter, "and to God the things that are God's" (Matt. 22:21). So we are to realize that this world's rules are binding and yet not the ultimate consideration.

Evangelical Response

While the evangelical means to abide by Jesus' teaching, he often suffers from the insensitive attitude of oth-

ers. Senator Mark Hatfield receives such criticism as reflected in these excerpts from two letters from constitu-
ents:

Why do you think you have the right to interfere with our
president? Have you forgotten that God's way is to respect and
honor those in authority?

I am in favor of shooting rioters that throw rocks from buildings
and try to force their wills upon others by violence.
    I and a lot of other Christian people are extremely disap-
pointed in your performance in the Senate, for you who claim
to be a Christian and have access to our Almighty God should
have a better understanding of human nature and the evil in
the human heart.[4]

Hatfield responds in two ways. First he points out what
seems to be the error in his critics' attack and then affirms
a positive course of action. We shall trace his line of
thinking as an evangelical case in point.

Hatfield calls into question the alignment of conservative theology with conservative social and political interests. There come to mind such political concessions as
printing "In God We Trust" on our currency and providing clergy for our military institutions. "But the political
establishment of religion means more than moral support," Peter Berger adds. "The writer strongly suspects
that the American state, by virtue of our tax-exemption
laws, gives more economic support to the churches than
European states in which religious establishments are still
legally recognized."[5] We create a political-religious alliance and treat the criticism of the one as an attack on the
other.

The product of such a union is common faith rather
than the evangelical faith. Note this comment: "I am the
most intensely religious man I know. That doesn't mean
that I adhere to any sect. A democracy cannot exist with-

out a religious base. I believe in democracy."[6] Such faith is real enough but uninformed by the gospel.

Hatfield next asks us to reevaluate the faith that we as a people have placed in the executive branch of the government.[7] "We should remind ourselves that our theological understanding of the nature of man means that excessive power resting with one person will likely be used for self-serving and self-justifying purposes," he warns, adding that "power shared by many—the premise of the democratic system—will more often be exercised with justice and wisdom."[8] Both our religious and our political traditions warn us against placing too much authority in the hands of a few.

Having witnessed the failure of his reform movements to gain public support, Jeremy Bentham confessed that man "prefers his own happiness to that of all other sentient beings put together."[9] Bentham's opinion may be an exaggerated one, but it alerts us to the need for a system of checks and balances.

The senator next asks us to recover a sense of the corporativeness of life: to sensitize ourselves to social as well as private morality; to respond to collective guilt in addition to individual guilt; to act in unison along with separate endeavor.

"A major fact of our civilization is that more and more sin becomes collective," Jacques Ellul observes, "and the individual is forced to participate in collective sin."[10]

If so, then the fruits of the Spirit should increasingly reflect a sense of corporate ministry and healing. The one-sided emphasis on private morality becomes the legalist's ploy to escape our more comprehensive responsibility.

Here we shift from Hatfield's rebuttal to his counterproposal. We pick up some of the priority concerns grow-

ing out of a healthy political conscience, and the first of
these deals with the persisting issue of peace and war.
"Blessed are the peacemakers," Jesus taught, "for they
shall be called sons of God" (Matt. 5:9). Hatfield allows
that his distaste for war grows out of a Christian conviction and that others might not be so motivated. "But I
cannot understand how a Christian community can abide
these evils without at least asking the questions which
need to be asked, and without at least coming to some
rudimentary and tentative responses to these questions."[11] Even the criterion of the traditional "just war"
doctrine requires that the means be consistent with the
ends being pursued.

The Senator was writing out of our agonizing experience with the conflict in Southeast Asia. He kept hearing
allusions to national pride and the avoidance of national
humiliation, to which he responded that "a nation that
can turn from its past ways, admit its error and truly seek
a new path, that nation can discover a true greatness of
spirit."[12] A people can rise from their knees to heights
that previously escaped them.

Hatfield believes that racial discrimination and oppression qualify as the second major political issue. Sherwood
Wirt takes a similar position: "The new evangelical is
weary of the subterfuges used to justify the preferential
treatment of one race over another. He finds it incredible
that anyone . . . should judge himself to be superior to
another person on the basis of racial origin."[13]

The evangelical means to press beyond revulsion to
action, both within and without the Christian community. The church should lead the way toward ending
social discrimination and act as a catalyst in a society
reluctant to accept the risks involved. "The evangelical
Christian of the new generation wants to apply the Bibli-

cal standard to bring social justice to racial minority groups. He does not have to be reminded that there are demonstrable inequalities among men, but he insists on going back to the premise that men have equal standing in the eyes of him who created them."[14]

Hatfield concludes his discussion of political projects with the inequitable distribution of wealth. There is a good deal of truth to the maxim that the rich get richer and the poor get poorer. Only some concerted effort will reverse the tendency.

The evangelical recalls that the Lord reached out to the unfortunate, even though this brought him into conflict with vested interests. It would be redundant to select incidents, for they characterized the Master's life, ministry, and teaching. The disciple can do no less than follow the precedent set in so forceful a manner.

The evangelical sets about to establish political priorities and exercise his stewardship. He believes that God will bless this course of action. He rests assured that such labor will not be in vain.

Realism and Hope

No one would mistake the evangelical for a utopian. He sees no simple solution to complex and persisting difficulties. He appreciates Reinhold Niebuhr's appraisal of the unrelenting task set before successive generations: "The problem which society faces is clearly one of reducing force by increasing the factors which make for a moral and rational adjustment to life, of bringing such force as is still necessary under responsibility of the whole society, of destroying the kind of power which cannot be made socially responsible . . . , and of bringing forces of moral restraint to power which can never be brought completely under social control."[15] The evangelical accepts the fact that his efforts inevitably meet with limited success.

In such a realistic framework, hope flourishes. The evangelical strives after a goal, a target, that helps him overreach himself. He imagines that hope can crack open those barriers erected by society and open up new opportunities for all. Hope resembles a political fantasy on the way to becoming a political reality.

How does the evangelical foster hope, seeing that circumstances often seem uncertain and contrary? He draws upon Scripture for the idea of "a new heaven and a new earth" (Rev. 21:1) to make him restless with his present accommodation. He also reads that "righteousness exalts a nation" (Prov. 14:34) as an admonition to revise the present political system.

Conversely, the evangelical imposes a proper restraint on his political vision. He withholds the ultimate solution to man's dilemma for the time when "the kingdom of the world has become the kingdom of our Lord, and of His Christ" (Rev. 11:15).

The evangelical rejects the temptation to retreat into some dream world and lose touch with our own. He refuses to become so heavenly-minded as to be of no earthly good.

But neither does the evangelical perspective produce an unbearable tension between our vision and reality as we experience it. It will not press us to falsify the situation in order to make the Christian faith appear more credible. It can sustain the reverses, face the stark realities left behind, and labor with the anticipation of God's blessing.

Finally, the evangelical derives hope from his identification with Christ. He remembers that Jesus pressed on in the face of the most discouraging of situations. The prophets had failed, opposition to Jesus' ministry had built up, the cross loomed against the horizon, but the Lord confidently went forcefully ahead.

With the resurrection morning came God's stamp of approval. Christ was raised from the dead and with him our hope for every subsequent situation in which we find ourselves.

"I have a dream that one day every valley shall be exalted, every hill and mountain shall be made low. The rough places will be made plain, and the crooked places will be made straight," Martin Luther King turns from a vision of the consummation to the hard realities of today. "This is the faith that I go back to the South with. With this faith we will be able to hew out of the mountain of despair a stone of hope. With this faith we will be able to work together, to pray together, to struggle together, to go to jail together, to stand up for freedom together, knowing we will be free one day."[16] He had a hope, cultivated by faith and translated into political action—much in the way the evangelical's political conscience operates in its better moments.

READER'S SUMMARY

Now to review some of the conclusions we have reached in broadening our understanding of the evangelical conscience:

1. The Scripture everywhere reflects God's interest in the political affairs of man. From such admonitions as may be implied in the extended family, through the prophets, to the injunctions of those who followed in Jesus' teaching, we observe the mandate to establish authority in order to curtail evil and extend the benefits of society.

2. We should not confuse religious and political com-

mitments, accept uncritically the judgment of those appointed to office, or ignore the corporate nature of life. These are the kind of traps which catch unsuspecting evangelicals.

3. Rather, we should focus on such pressing social issues as war, racial discrimination, and the inequitable distribution of wealth. We ought to take on those vexing problems which plague mankind and not get sidetracked by partisan rhetoric.

4. The evangelical expects no easy resolution of such problems but believes that he can render a meaningful service. The Scripture puts a proper restraint on our political visions, thus leaving the ultimate solution in God's hand and in his time.

5. But Scripture does incite us to hope. It keeps the future open to the marvelous things that God may be pleased to accomplish through us. Christ has so kindled this hope in our hearts that it cannot be snuffed out.

6. Faith must be translated into political action. The evangelical is gaining an increased appreciation for his political role, for some as a vocation and for all as an informed and active constituency. He cannot reserve his efforts for the world to come when Jesus invested so thoroughly in the world that now exists.

In the Cultural Context

We round out our discussion of the evangelical conscience with a consideration of culture. The term "culture" signifies something distinctively human. Man is
similar to animals in some respects but transcends them
in others.

Emil Brunner labors the distinction: "The impulse to
create the beautiful, to realize justice, to know the truth,
to preserve the past, to enter into spiritual communica-
tions, to invent the new, to extend the range of interhu-
man communion to share the sufferings and joys of others; the impulse to submit the totality of life to ultimate
directives and give it a meaning, unity and intelligibility,
and finally to place everything under the divine will and
receive it from the hands of God—all these are impulses
out of which culture and civilization arise."[1]

"Man is unique," Leslie White concurs. "He is the
only living species that has a culture. . . . Specifically and
concretely culture consists of tools, implements, utensils,
clothing, ornaments, customs, institutions, beliefs, ritu-
als, games, works of art, language, etc."[2]

Several years ago I stood at an excavation site in northern Israel and viewed the remains of an ancient civilization. What appeared to be a human skull, some broken
potsherds, and a stone artifact gave evidence that man

had settled there previously. Culture reflects man's attempts to make the world a home to live in. It may take the form of a village hut or a great cathedral, but each represents alike the human saga.

THE CRITICAL ALTERNATIVE

Although we observe such a great variety in human expression, one decision lies at the heart of man's cultural enterprise: "either to continue along this road of the modern age, the road of emancipation from the Christian truth which leads to the total effacement of anything truly human and perhaps even to its complete physical annihilation, *or* to go back to the source of justice, truth and love, which is the God of justice, truth and love in whom only lies the power of salvation."[3]

Culture reflects man's response to his Maker. Let God drop out of the enterprise and culture degenerates and totters on the brink of oblivion. Contemporary man faces just this pressing possibility.

In his quest for culture, man's motives "are mixed with egoism, lust for power, and ambition."[4] It is as though there were unleashed in man every sort of wild destructive tendency that would frustrate his cultural endeavor. God instructed man to master the earth, but man has failed to control even himself.

The only solution to man's dilemma is to return to God and to the place of a responsible stewardship for creation. It is to "go back to the source of justice, truth and love" (ingredients of the cultural task) by way of God "in whom only lies the power of salvation." Brunner puts the condition in the most uncompromising fashion, and the evangelical applauds him for doing so.

THE EVANGELICAL THRUST

We pick up the evangelical train of thought by shifting our emphasis from Brunner's initial comments to the perspective developed by the seventeenth-century bishop and educator, John Amos Comenius. He urged that it is man's responsibility to pursue learning (know oneself), virtue (control oneself), and piety (relate to the Almighty). "In these three things is situated the whole excellence of man, for they alone are the foundation of the present and of the future life. All other things (health, strength, beauty, riches, honour, friendship, good-fortune, long life) are as nothing, if God grant them to any, but extrinsic ornaments of life, and if a man greedily grope after them, engross himself in their pursuit, occupy and overwhelm himself with them to the neglect of those more important matters, then they become superfluous vanities and harmful obstructions."[5]

The evangelical sees the pursuit of learning as an important feature of our cultural creativity. "Particular analyses and world views may be unacceptable to the Christian and may create problems for him, but he will still be compelled to think both critically and systematically," Arthur Holmes concludes. "Such is inevitable in mature and alert, committed and responsible individuals; and it becomes a special obligation for those who seek to harness every ability for the glory of God."[6] The Christian cherishes all truth as God's truth.

This conclusion will no doubt seem strange to those accustomed to thinking of the evangelical as close-minded. Such a notion arises in part from the zeal of the evangelical in contending for the truth. "The type of religion which rejoices in the pious sound of traditional phrases, regardless of their meanings, or shrinks from 'controversial' matters will never stand amid the shocks of life."[7] The evangelical assumes a more rigorous course in his search for truth.

The fundamentalist/modernist controversy also raised the possibility that the evangelical might be prejudiced against new insights. However, the fact is that colleges and seminaries were compromising their commitment to the gospel. Young people from evangelical homes went away to school only to lose their faith. Young seminarians became increasingly out of touch with their evangelical constituency. As a result, the evangelical became wary of education that undermined the Christian conviction.

But the evangelical's commitment to learning did not waver in the face of the onslaught on his faith. He broke off from the existing institutions and established Bible institutes, colleges, and seminaries that would promote Christian propositions.

The evangelical does not think of knowledge as an end in itself, but as a means of attaining virtue. It presses us to make responsible decisions as the stewards of life. For instance, Leroy Augenstein poses the possibility of extending the life of an ailing grandparent through a kidney transplant. "Doctor, I realize that I'm asking you to play God, but we need your advice very much," the petition began, adding that "if I don't do what I can to save his life, I'll never forgive myself. Yet if I do give up one of my kidneys I may be cheating myself and my own family."[8] There was a good chance that the operation would increase the duration of life for at least a year, perhaps two or three, five at the most. Certainly not a gift to be taken lightly!

However, they estimated that the loss of a kidney would reduce the grandson's life expectancy by as much

as ten years, provided that no really significant technolog-
ical developments were to come along in the interim.
Now the decision seemed to weigh against the operation.

Still the grandfather was an outstanding surgeon whose
skill saved hundreds of lives each year. He served in addition a large, remote area, where there had been no success
in securing a replacement for him. Should these facts
have altered the decision? Would it make any difference
if one knew that the grandson had a two-year-old daugh-
ter, that his wife was pregnant, or that he was a promising
graduate student in medical research?

Augenstein was not actually asked to play God, as
suggested in the request, but to assume his full role as
man. He had to render advice, no matter how difficult it
became, on the basis of conflicting evidence and what
good he might hope to accomplish.

The evangelical's idea of virtue steers between the
denial and the abuse of our capacities. One alternative
asks man to set aside his peculiar prerogatives and sit
complacently by regardless of what may come to pass.
"Rather, the proper utilization of our new scientific
findings requires that we face up to some terribly critical
decisions, based upon our most fundamental values and
beliefs."[9] We do not reject the pace of scientific discovery or allow our perspective to lag behind; we use our
insights thoughtfully, sensitively, and devoutly.

The evangelical supposes that in order to employ
knowledge wisely we must cultivate a relationship to the
Almighty. "A Christian view of education . . . has at its
very center the transformation and restoration of the
person estranged from God."[10] There we tap "the source
of justice, truth and love . . . in whom only lies the power
of salvation."

The evangelical repudiates the deist's idea that God set

the creation in motion with the cultural mandate and let man take over at that point. The Almighty sustains the world by his grace and ministers to those who seek to further their cultural obligations. Life consists in an ongoing communion with God and cooperative endeavor.

What is the nature of our cultural enterprise? To pursue learning, virtue, and piety and so transcend the mere demand of organic necessity. To satisfy "the impulse to create the beautiful, to realize justice, to know the truth, to preserve the past, . . . to place everything under the divine will and receive it from the hands of God."

THE TEST

A vital and vigorous church is the first evidence that we are fulfilling the cultural mandate. More specifically, the church must be able to recall the mandate, celebrate its importance, and act responsibly in connection with it.

We ought not to expect the world to keep the commands of God clearly in mind. "For even though they knew God," Paul described the course of human events, "they did not honor Him as God, or give thanks" (Rom. 1:21). Man has a chronically short memory so far as God is concerned.

But the church should be an exception. It is a fellowship meant to review the purposes that God has for mankind. It is deliberately committed to the study of Scripture and its application to life. It takes "into account God's original charge [to subdue the earth] which has been called man's cultural mandate, and affirms that in Christ as Lord of all, this mandate takes on new significance for the Christian."[11]

The church ought also to greet the cultural mandate with enthusiasm. Its worship strikes a note of festivity and its ministry echoes a joyous refrain: "The lines have fallen to me in pleasant places; indeed, my heritage is beautiful to me" (Ps. 16:6).

"Take My yoke upon you," Jesus charged the disciples, "for My yoke is easy, and My load is light" (Matt. 11:29–30). Those previously burdened with an oppressive weight derived comfort and delight from the Master's injunction.

Finally, the church fulfills the cultural mandate through service. It is a fellowship where "men and women discover new possibilities for creative thought and action."[12] A case in point relates to the civil rights bill of 1964. This was the first time in American history, so far as I can determine, that a single Protestant, Eastern Orthodox, Roman Catholic, and Jewish testimony was presented to Congress in support of legislation. The testimonial drew upon a common Biblical heritage to rectify the situation at hand.

However, the church is but one institution among many. The second barometer of our responsiveness to the cultural mandate is how well our social institutions in general minister to human need.

Some years ago I attempted to get assistance for a hard-pressed family in an urban area. The husband had deserted his wife and children, leaving them in a condemned building. The city shut off the water for the building, so that the family had to secure their supply from sympathetic neighbors. They had no central heat and depended on a gas range to cut the bite of the winter's cold. Several of the children were pathetically ill. Such aid as the family received was inadequate and often tardy in arriving.

My efforts on behalf of the family proved frustrating in the face of political red tape, overly burdened community services, and persons not willing to get involved. Our institutions fell critically short of the obligation implied by the cultural mandate.

The third clue to cultural responsibility relates to the ideas and perspectives generated by a given society. These may be influenced by the professionals in their varied fields or from a wider ground swell of public opinion.

"The authentic literary artist seeks for meaning and pattern in the midst of the changing and the relative," writes Beatrice Batson of the professional's role in forming cultural concepts, "and discloses in his own aesthetic way truth about God, man and the world."[13] His expertise provides the channel for revealing an understanding of the world in which we live and how he anticipates that we should meet that challenge.

On the other hand, "the distinguishing feature [of man's culture] is the elevation of popular taste and conviction to an effectively unchallenged supremacy."[14] It overrides the refinements of the professional in order to further some generally preferred option.

Whether we qualify as a professional in some field of specialization or not, each person can influence to a certain degree the prevailing point of view. The result may appear incidental, but it is a factor to be taken seriously. And the cumulative result helps to measure our obedience to the cultural mandate.

The psalmist's warning seems an appropriate conclusion to the matter:

> Do not harden your hearts, as at Meribah,
> As in the day of Massah in the wilderness;
> "When your fathers tested Me,
> They tried Me, though they had seen My work."
> (Ps. 95:8–9)

We ought not to take God's commands lightly, as though we had no understanding of his desire to instill righteousness in the hearts of men. We should weave the fabric of society so as to please the Giver of Life.

READER'S SUMMARY

We turn now to review the points covered in this final discussion:

1. Culture is the distinctively human enterprise. It reflects man's quest for meaning, as a unique creature of God bent on estimating his place in the universe. It "is what man uniquely does as he attempts to make the world a home to live in."

2. The evangelical's attitude toward culture resembles that of John Amos Comenius, who saw culture as the result of man's pursuit of learning, virtue, and piety. The evangelical has a high regard for the exercise of reason in that he assumes that all truth is God's truth.

3. However, the evangelical is never satisfied with knowledge alone, for every gift implies its responsible use. Beyond learning lies the virtue we must exercise through a difficult decision-making process.

4. As a result, we are reminded of our vital relationship to God in the cultural endeavor. The evangelical means to cultivate the Source of the beautiful, justice, and truth. He views the reverence of God as the beginning and end of culture and so adds piety to learning and virtue.

5. The objective measurements of culture are a vigorous ecclesiastical, institutional, and conceptual endeavor (not that we can separate one from the other except for purposes of analysis). The church provides the only adequate context in which the cultural mandate can be "recalled, honored, and acted upon." It has the memory,

capacity for celebration, and anticipation to solicit the interest of others.

6. The Christian conscience can therefore play a significant role in forming a social pattern and implementing its goals. It may weigh the conventional ideas and institutions as to how well they accommodate the teaching of Scripture. In view of preserving the valuable aspects of our cultural legacy, it seeks to renew what has lapsed, or call into being some creative alternatives.

7. The evangelical concludes that his faith bears on all of life. There are no genuinely *secular* areas. Jesus is Lord of all!

Notes

1. EVANGELICAL TERRAIN

1. Donald Bloesch, *The Evangelical Renaissance*, p. 13.
2. Karl Barth, *The Humanity of God*, p. 11.
3. See Bernard Ramm, *The Evangelical Heritage*, pp. 11–21, for a discussion of the evangelical legacy from the Western church.
4. James C. Livingston, *Modern Christian Thought*, p. 1.
5. Peter Gay, *The Enlightenment*, Vol. I, p. 24.
6. Friedrich Schleiermacher, *On Religion: Speeches to Its Cultural Despisers*, p. 28.
7. Compare with L. Harold DeWolf, *The Case for Theology in Liberal Perspective*, and Henry P. Van Dusen, *The Vindication of Liberal Theology*, as sympathetic treatments of the liberal tradition.
8. Eldred Vanderlaan (ed.), *Fundamentalism Versus Modernism*, p. 56.
9. Review Ramm, *The Evangelical Heritage*, pp. 23–63, in the light of the above statement.
10. Dean M. Kelley, *Why Conservative Churches Are Growing*, pp. vi–viii.

2. APPEAL TO GOD THE FATHER

1. William Hordern, *A Layman's Guide to Protestant Theology*, p. 57. Hordern uses the phrase "fundamentalist and conservative," which I take to be roughly synonymous with my understanding of the term "evangelical."
2. *Ibid.*, p. 2.
3. *Ibid.*, p. 10.
4. The *evangelical faith* may also be thought of as at the heart of

155

Christian orthodoxy, but then in reference to content rather than a revived commitment.

5. Gardiner Day, *The Apostles' Creed*, p. 115.

6. Christian orthodoxy would subsequently find it proper and indeed necessary to spell out the nature of Trinitarian faith. Controversy often resulted, along with the failure to reach a consensus, as in the case of whether the Holy Spirit may be said to proceed from Father and Son or from Father alone.

7. John Burnaby, *The Belief of Christendom*, p. 20.

8. *Ibid.*, p. 25.

9. The term "sinner" here relates to the irreligious, the immoral, or both. While we all qualify as sinners in one sense, its use in the Gospels is largely restricted to this more selective meaning.

10. J. Edwin Orr, *Faith That Makes Sense*, p. 14.

11. Burnaby, *The Belief of Christendom*, p. 39.

3. WITNESS TO JESUS CHRIST

1. John Reumann writing in the introduction to Joachim Jeremias, *The Problem of the Historical Jesus*, pp. ix–x.

2. Albert Schweitzer, *The Quest of the Historical Jesus*, p. 401.

3. Jeremias, *The Problem of the Historical Jesus*, p. xv.

4. Burnaby, *The Belief of Christendom*, p. 87. Burnaby does not look in favor on making belief in the virgin birth a theological test case. "No one saw or could see it happen," he argues, "no one can describe or explain how it was possible" (p. 84). However, the evangelical is seldom inclined to write the issue off so readily. He has a good deal of sympathy for William Jennings Bryan's commentary: "The virgin birth is no more mysterious than the birth of each of us—it is simply different. No one without revelation has ever solved the mystery of life, whether it be the life found in man, or in the beast or in the plant. The God who can give life can certainly give it in any way or through any means that may please Him" (Vanderlaan, ed., *Fundamentalism Versus Modernism*, p. 24). Of course, no one saw it happen, but if God reveals the matter, why hedge on it? Unless, as Bryan suspects, some naturalistic prejudice is creeping in around the corners of our conviction.

5. Helmut Thielicke, *I Believe*, p. 84.

6. *Ibid.*, p. 133.

7. This figure is most clearly explored in Eph. 4:7–13 but seems to

underlie much of the apostle's thinking.

8. Morris A. Inch, *Paced by God*, p. 84.

9. The "session" refers to Christ's place of authority from which he intercedes on behalf of those trusting in him.

4. ACCENT ON THE HOLY SPIRIT

1. Thielicke, *I Believe*, p. 31.

2. Burnaby, *The Belief of Christendom*, p. 128.

3. Thielicke, *I Believe*, p. 226.

4. This perspective anticipates the remainder of the Creed: how that the Holy Spirit means to complete the task of redeeming the total man in his entire situation.

5. Day, *The Apostles' Creed*, p. 122.

6. Inch, *Paced by God*, p. 114.

7. Millard Erickson, *The New Evangelical Theology*, p. 117.

8. Day, *The Apostles' Creed*, p. 142.

9. *Ibid.*, p. 147.

10. Oscar Cullmann, *Immortality of the Soul or Resurrection of the Dead?* p. 25.

11. John Kelley, *Early Christian Creeds*, p. 387.

12. Barth, *The Humanity of God*, p. 19.

5. THE CENTRALITY OF SCRIPTURE

1. Hordern, *A Layman's Guide to Protestant Theology*, p. 59.

2. Vanderlaan (ed.), *Fundamentalism Versus Modernism*, p.32.

3. James Packer, *Fundamentalism and the Word of God*, p. 54. "As well as endorsing the principle of biblical authority in its application to others," Packer elaborates, "our Lord submitted to it Himself. He read the Old Testament as the word of His Father. His mind was saturated in it, as His teaching showed. He met the tempter by avowing His intention to obey what was written. He kept the law. . . . His whole ministry may be described as a prolonged and many-sided affirmation of the authority of the Old Testament" (pp. 56, 57).

4. Kenneth S. Kantzer, "The Authority of the Bible," in Merrill C. Tenney (ed.), *The Word for This Century*, p. 50.

5. Packer, *Fundamentalism and the Word of God*, p. 63.

6. Hordern, *A Layman's Guide to Protestant Theology*, p. 57.

7. *Ibid.*, p. 59.

8. Paul Tillich writes concerning this movement: "Orthodox theology was and still is the solid basis of all later developments, whether these developments . . . were directed against orthodoxy, or were attempts at restoration of it" (*A History of Christian Thought*, p. 276).

9. Fundamentalism was not a monolithic development. Ernest H. Sandeen mentions the role that dispensationalism and the Princeton theology played, adding that "the two movements were by no means completely compatible, but the common Modernist foe kept them at peace with one another throughout the nineteenth and early twentieth centuries" (*The Origins of Fundamentalism*, p. 14).

10. William Chillingworth, *The Religion of Protestants*, p. 463.

11. Alan Stibbs, *Understanding God's Word*, p. 32.

12. Ramm, *The Evangelical Heritage*, p. 30.

13. Robert Dick Wilson, *A Scientific Investigation of the Old Testament*, p. 213.

14. Kantzer, "The Authority of the Bible," in Tenney (ed.), pp. 34–51.

15. Bernard Ramm, *The Christian View of Science and Scripture*, p. 66.

6. EVANGELISM

1. Hordern, *A Layman's Guide to Protestant Theology*, p. 48.

2. Bloesch, *The Evangelical Renaissance*, p. 48.

3. Carl F. H. Henry, "Man's Dilemma: Sin," in Tenney (ed.), *The Word for This Century*, p. 8.

4. Erickson, *The New Evangelical Theology*, p. 104.

5. Ramm, *The Evangelical Heritage*, p. 149.

6. John Stott, "The Bible Basis of Evangelism," in J. D. Douglas (ed.), *Let the Earth Hear His Voice*, p. 67.

7. Douglas (ed.), *Let the Earth Hear His Voice*, p. 3. The significant preface of the Lausanne Covenant, affirmed in July of 1974, reads as follows: "We, members of the Church of Jesus Christ, from more than 150 nations, participants in the International Congress on World Evangelism at Lausanne, praise God for his great salvation and rejoice in the fellowship he has given us with himself and with each other. We are deeply stirred by what God is doing in our day, moved to penitence by our failures and challenged by the unfinished task of evangelization. We believe the Gospel is God's good news for the whole world, and we are determined by his grace to obey Christ's

commission to proclaim it to all mankind and to make disciples of every nation. We desire, therefore, to affirm our faith and our resolve, and to make public our covenant." The statement has subsequently been signed by individuals and congregations around the world as an evangelical commitment to world evangelism.

8. Stott, "The Bible Basis of Evangelism," in Douglas (ed.), pp. 70–71.

9. Inch, *Paced by God,* p. 69.

10. The evangelical holds that God chose Israel as a peculiar people. No nation can presume to substitute its own history for that of the patriarchs and prophets.

11. Erickson, *The New Evangelical Theology,* p. 112.

12. Stott, "The Bible Basis of Evangelism," in Douglas (ed.), p. 69.

13. Hordern, *A Layman's Guide to Protestant Theology,* p. 65.

14. Stott, "The Bible Basis of Evangelism," in Douglas (ed.), p. 71.

7. MISSIONS

1. Elisabeth Elliot, *Through Gates of Splendor,* p. 18.

2. Ralph Winter, "The Highest Priority: Cross-Cultural Evangelism," in Douglas (ed.), *Let the Earth Hear His Voice,* pp. 213–225.

3. *Ibid.,* p. 218.

4. Douglas (ed.), *Let the Earth Hear His Voice,* p. 6.

5. Winter, "The Highest Priority: Cross-Cultural Evangelism," in Douglas (ed.), p. 221.

6. I suspect that the success of Youth for Christ, Campus Crusade, and Inter-Varsity Christian Fellowship (as evangelical cases in point) could in substantial measure be explained as instances of E-2 evangelism.

7. J. Herbert Kane, *Understanding Christian Missions,* pp. 95–96.

8. *Ibid.,* p. 95.

9. H. Richard Niebuhr's *Christ and Culture* is the theological primer on the subject. Especially as he relates the options of Christ against culture, Christ of culture, Christ and culture in paradox, and Christ the transformer of culture.

10. Emil Brunner, *Christianity and Civilisation,* Vol. II, p. 131.

11. *Ibid.*

12. Julian Hartt, *The Lost Image of Man,* pp. 34–35.

13. Douglas (ed.), *Let the Earth Hear His Voice,* p. 7.

8. How Evangelicals View Themselves

1. Kenneth Scott Latourette, *A History of the Expansion of Christianity*, Vol. I, p. 170.

2. Morris A. Inch, "The Place of the Incarnation in Biblical Interpretation," in Samuel J. Schultz and Morris A. Inch (eds.), *Interpreting the Word of God*, p. 166.

3. Latourette, *A History of the Expansion of Christianity*, Vol. I, p. 368.

4. Bloesch, *The Evangelical Renaissance*, p. 70.

5. Ned Stonehouse, *J. Gresham Machen*, p. 187.

6. Sandeen, *The Origins of Fundamentalism*, p. 5. Dispensationalism refers to the division of time into periods of dispensations corresponding to the ground rules God designs for each instance. *The Schofield Reference Bible* identified seven in all: Innocence (the Garden of Eden), Conscience (Adam to Noah), Human Government (Noah to Abraham), Promise (Abraham to Moses), Law (Moses to Christ), Grace (Christ through the judgment), and the Kingdom (Millennium).

7. Billy Graham, "Christ in the Believer," in Tenney (ed.), *The Word for This Century*, p. 92.

8. The haggada were rabbinical legends, narratives, or expositions.

9. Ramm, *The Evangelical Heritage*, p. 155.

10. It seems impossible to suggest a good reading list to cover the wide variety of evangelicals today. My own practice is to recommend upon consultation with the interested individual. The alternative of a standard list has so far as I am concerned proved ineffective and even misleading.

11. Killian McDonnell, quoted in Richard Quebedeaux, *The Young Evangelicals*, p. 1.

9. In Regard to Ecumenical Concerns

1. Edward John Carnell, *The Case for Biblical Christianity*, ed. by Ronald H. Nash, p. 13.

2. Ramm, *The Evangelical Heritage*, p. 152.

3. J. Marcellus Kik, *Ecumenism and the Evangelical*, p. 101.

4. Vernon Grounds, "The Biblical Basis of Christian Unity," in W. Stanley Mooneyham (ed.), *The Dynamics of Christian Unity*, p. 35.

5. *Ibid.*, p. 36.

6. *Ibid.*, p. 38.

7. Earle E. Cairns, "Ecumenism in the Light of Chruch History," in Mooneyham (ed.), pp. 53–65.

8. Ignatius, Ephesians 2.

9. Ignatius, Trallians 3, Smyrnaeans 8.

10. Ignatius, Philadelphians 4.

11. Cairns, "Ecumenism in the Light of Church History," in Mooneyham (ed.), p. 56.

12. Bloesch, *The Evangelical Renaissance*, p. 29.

10. In Regard to Social Action

1. Earle E. Cairns, *The Christian in Society*, p. 162.

2. Erickson, *The New Evangelical Theology*, p. 178.

3. The Roman Catholic fundamentalists had an easier time of it, at least at the outset, given the support of the church hierarchy. Nevertheless, the ferment continued within the Roman communion, as did suspicion and more gradual but persistent energy drain.

4. Carl F. H. Henry, *Aspects of Christian Social Ethics*, p. 15.

5. *Ibid.*, p. 17.

6. Cairns, *The Christian in Society*, p. 120.

7. *Ibid.*, p. 121.

8. *Ibid.*, p. 124.

9. *Ibid.*, p. 130.

10. *Ibid.*, p. 137.

11. Bloesch, *The Evangelical Renaissance*, p. 29.

12. Sherwood Wirt, *The Social Conscience of the Evangelical*, p. 53.

13. Ramm, *The Evangelical Heritage*, p. 140.

14. Henry, *Aspects of Christian Social Ethics*, p. 129.

15. Wirt, *The Social Conscience of the Evangelical*, p. 2.

11. In the Political Arena

1. Inch, *Paced by God*, p. 106.

2. *Ibid.*

3. *Ibid.*, p. 107.

4. Mark O. Hatfield, *Conflict and Conscience*, p. 22.

5. Peter Berger, *The Noise of Solemn Assemblies*, pp. 61–62.

6. *Ibid.*, p. 63.

7. It is striking that Senator Hatfield's warning came long before our

confidence was jolted by the Watergate affair. The events have justified the concern he expressed at an earlier time.

8. Hatfield, *Conflict and Conscience*, p. 27.

9. Jeremy Bentham, *Works*, Vol. X, p. 80.

10. Jacques Ellul, *The Presence of the Kingdom*, p. 13.

11. Hatfield, *Conflict and Conscience*, p. 29.

12. *Ibid.*

13. Wirt, *The Social Conscience of the Evangelical*, p. 81.

14. *Ibid.*, pp. 80–81.

15. Reinhold Niebuhr, *Moral Man and Immoral Society*, p. 20.

16. Charles Osborne (ed.), *I Have a Dream*, p. 57.

12.   IN THE CULTURAL CONTEXT

1. Brunner, *Christianity and Civilisation*, Vol. II, p. 128.

2. Leslie A. White, *The Evolution of Culture*, p. 3.

3. Brunner, *Christianity and Civilisation*, Vol. I, p. 158.

4. *Ibid.*, Vol. II, p. 128.

5. Keatinge (ed.), *Comenius*, p. 24.

6. Arthur F. Holmes, "Philosophy," in Hudson T. Armerding (ed.), *Christianity and the World of Thought*, p. 57.

7. J. Gresham Machen, *Christianity and Liberalism*, p. 1.

8. Leroy Augenstein, *Come, Let Us Play God*, p. 1.

9. *Ibid.*, p. 3.

10. Cornelius Jaarsma, "Education," in Armerding (ed.), p. 111.

11. *Ibid.*

12. John C. Bennett (ed.), *Christian Social Ethics in a Changing World*, p. 35.

13. Beatrice Batson, "The Christian and Modern Literature," in Armerding (ed.), p. 50.

14. Julian Hartt, *A Christian Critique of American Culture*, p. 391.

Bibliography

Armerding, Hudson T. (ed.). *Christianity and the World of Thought.* Moody Press, 1968.

Augenstein, Leroy. *Come, Let Us Play God.* Harper & Row, Publishers, Inc., 1969.

Barth, Karl. *The Humanity of God.* John Knox Press, 1960.

Bennett, John C. (ed.). *Christian Social Ethics in a Changing World.* Association Press, 1966.

Bentham, Jeremy. *Works.* Edinburgh: Tait, 1843.

Berger, Peter. *The Noise of Solemn Assemblies.* Doubleday & Company, Inc., 1961.

Bloesch, Donald. *The Evangelical Renaissance.* Wm. B. Eerdmans Publishing Company, 1973.

Brunner, Emil. *Christianity and Civilisation.* 2 vols. London: James Nisbet & Co., Ltd., 1947.

Burnaby, John. *The Belief of Christendom.* London: S.P.C.K., 1959.

Cairns, Earle E. *The Christian in Society.* Moody Press, 1973.

Carnell, Edward John. *The Case for Biblical Christianity*, ed. by Ronald H. Nash. Wm. B. Eerdmans Publishing Company, 1969.

Chillingworth, William. *The Religion of Protestants.* London: Bell and Daldy, 1870.

Cullmann, Oscar. *Immortality of the Soul or Resurrection of the Dead?* London: The Epworth Press, 1958.

Day, Gardiner. *The Apostles' Creed.* Charles Scribner's Sons, 1963.

DeWolf, L. Harold. *The Case for Theology in Liberal Perspective.* The Westminster Press, 1959.

Douglas, J. D. (ed.). *Let the Earth Hear His Voice.* World Wide Publications, 1975.

Elliot, Elisabeth. *Through Gates of Splendor.* Harper & Brothers, 1957.

Ellul, Jacques. *The Presence of the Kingdom,* tr. by Olive Wyon. The Westminster Press, 1952.

Erickson, Millard. *The New Evangelical Theology.* Fleming H. Revell Company, 1968.

Gay, Peter. *The Enlightenment.* 2 vols. Alfred A. Knopf, Inc., 1966, 1969.

Hartt, Julian. *A Christian Critique of American Culture.* Harper & Row, Publishers, Inc., 1967.

———. *The Lost Image of Man.* Louisiana State University Press, 1963.

Hatfield, Mark O. *Conflict and Conscience.* Word, Inc., 1971.

Henry, Carl F. H. *Aspects of Christian Social Ethics.* Wm. B. Eerdmans Publishing Company, 1964.

Hordern, William. *A Layman's Guide to Protestant Theology.* The Macmillan Company, 1955.

Ignatius. *The Epistles. The Apostolic Fathers,* tr. by Kirsopp Lake. 2 vols. Cambridge: Harvard University, 1912.

Inch, Morris A. *Paced by God.* Word, Inc., 1973.

Jeremias, Joachim. *The Problem of the Historical Jesus.* Fortress Press, 1964.

Kane, J. Herbert. *Understanding Christian Missions.* Baker Book House, 1974.

Keatinge, M. W. (ed.). *Comenius.* McGraw-Hill Book Co., Inc., 1931.

Kelley, Dean M. *Why Conservative Churches Are Growing.* Harper & Row, Publishers, Inc., 1972.

Kelley, John. *Early Christian Creeds.* London: Longmans, Green & Company, Ltd., 1964.

Kik, J. Marcellus. *Ecumenism and the Evangelical.* Presbyterian & Reformed Publishing Co., 1958.

Latourette, Kenneth Scott. *A History of the Expansion of Christianity.* 7 vols. Harper & Brothers, 1937–1945.

Livingston, James C. *Modern Christian Thought.* The Macmillan Company, 1971.

Machen, J. Gresham. *Christianity and Liberalism.* Wm. B. Eerdmans Publishing Company, 1923.

Mooneyham, W. Stanley (ed.). *The Dynamics of Christian Unity.* Zondervan Publishing House, 1963.

Nelson, J. Robert. *The Realm of Redemption.* London: Epworth Press, 1951.

Niebuhr, H. Richard. *Christ and Culture.* Harper & Brothers, 1951.

Niebuhr, Reinhold. *Moral Man and Immoral Society.* Charles Scribner's Sons, 1960.

Orr, J. Edwin. *Faith That Makes Sense.* Judson Press, 1960.

Osborne, Charles (ed.). *I Have a Dream.* Time-Life Books, 1968.

Packer, James. *Fundamentalism and the Word of God.* Wm. B. Eerdmans Publishing Company, 1958.

Quebedeaux, Richard. *The Young Evangelicals.* Harper & Row, Publishers, Inc., 1974.

Ramm, Bernard. *The Christian View of Science and Scripture.* Wm. B. Eerdmans Publishing Company, 1954.

_____. *The Evangelical Heritage.* Word, Inc., 1973.

Sandeen, Ernest H. *The Origins of Fundamentalism.* Fortress Press, 1968.

Schleiermacher, Friedrich. *On Religion: Speeches to Its Cultured Despisers,* tr. by John Oman. Harper & Brothers, 1958.

Schultz, Samuel J., and Inch, Morris A. (eds.). *Interpreting the Word of God.* Moody Press, 1976.

Schweitzer, Albert. *The Quest of the Historical Jesus.* London: Black, 1910.

Stibbs, Alan. *Understanding God's Word.* London: Inter-Varsity Fellowship, 1962.

Stonehouse, Ned. *J. Gresham Machen.* Wm. B. Eerdmans Publishing Company, 1954.

Tenney, Merrill C. (ed.). *The Word for This Century.* Oxford University Press, 1960.

Thielicke, Helmut. *I Believe,* tr. by John W. Doberstein and H. George Anderson. Fortress Press, 1968.

Van Dusen, Henry P. *The Vindication of Liberal Theology.* Charles Scribner's Sons, 1963.

Vanderlaan, Eldred (ed.). *Fundamentalism Versus Modernism.* New York: Wilson, 1925.

White, Leslie A. *The Evolution of Culture.* McGraw-Hill Book Co., Inc., 1959.

Willis, Geoffrey. *Saint Augustine and the Donatist Controversy.* London: S.P.C.K., 1950.

Wilson, Robert Dick. *A Scientific Investigation of the Old Testament.* Philadelphia: Sunday School Times, 1926.

Wirt, Sherwood. *The Social Conscience of the Evangelical.* Harper & Row, Publishers, Inc., 1968.